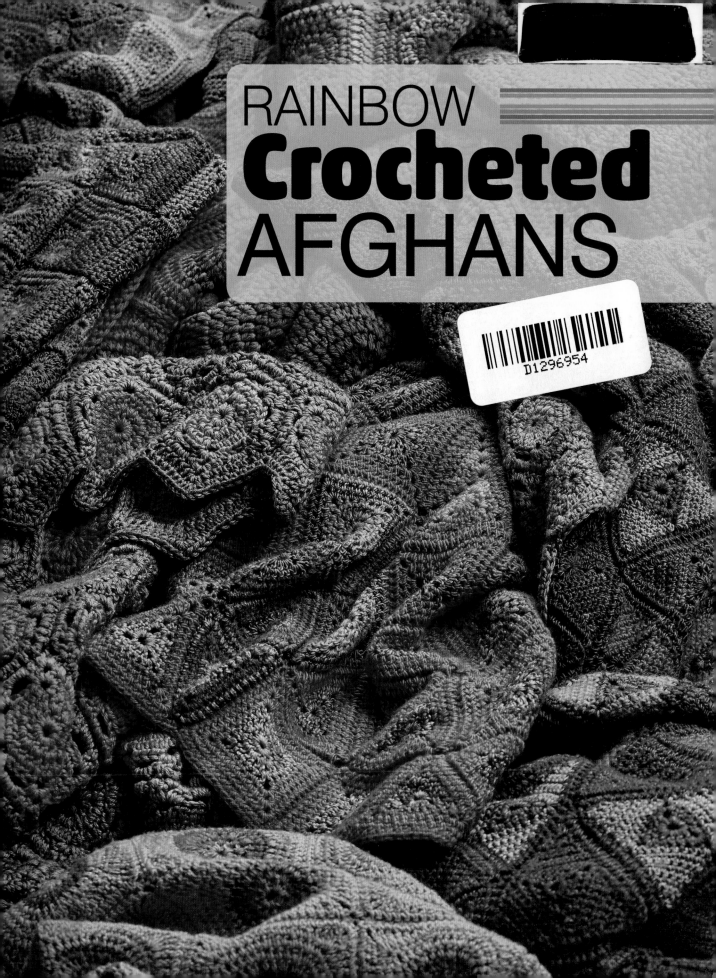

RAINBOW
Crocheted
AFGHANS

RAINBOW
Crocheted
AFGHANS

A BLOCK-BY-BLOCK GUIDE TO CREATING COLORFUL BLANKETS AND THROWS

Amanda Perkins

SEARCH PRESS

First published in 2016

Search Press Limited
Wellwood, North Farm Road,
Tunbridge Wells, Kent TN2 3DR

Illustrations and text copyright © Amanda Perkins 2016

Photographs by Roddy Paine Photographic Studio

Photographs and design copyright © Search Press Limited 2016

ISBN: 978-1-78221-438-0

The Publishers and author can accept no responsibility for any consequences arising from the information, advice or instructions given in this publication.

Suppliers
If you have difficulty in obtaining any of the materials and equipment mentioned in this book, then please visit the Search Press website for details of suppliers:
www.searchpress.com

www.amandascrochetblog.blogspot.co.uk

Printed in China

Dedication

This book is dedicated to the three women in my life who have inspired and taught me. To my Granny and Mother – who have both sadly passed away – I'm sure they would approve and be proud of their influence, and to my beloved Aunty Pat who is still sewing and creating and inspiring.

Acknowledgements

To Valerie – for her encouragement and advice, and her never-ending support both as my technical editor and friend.

Extra special thanks to my husband Phil and daughter Daisy for their never-ending love and encouragement – they persuaded me that writing a book was a good idea in the first place and then suffered the consequences.

To Felice and Fred, who have shaped me as a person and always lived happily with a slightly obsessive and distracted mum. And to my Dad and the rest of my long-suffering family – who don't always understand, but have always supported me from the sidelines.

To Joy from The Knitting Goddess, who kindly dyed some of the colors for my color wheel.

And finally to my three animals – who have no idea what's going on, but kept me company and gave me somebody to talk to during the long, solitary hours spent crocheting ten afghans.

Contents

Introduction

I come from a long family line of people who have worked with textiles: my great-great-grandmother and my great-grandmother were both seamstresses; my granny knitted, crocheted and even made her own carpets, while my grandad was an upholsterer and sewed wings for flying boats during World War II – it is also rumored that he crocheted as well. Both my mother and aunt sewed all their own clothes, and when they weren't sewing they knitted and crocheted!

I studied for a diploma at Art College, specializing in textiles; my final project was a giant knitted intarsia poncho inspired by Aztec design. After this, I spent several years making patchwork quilts but I never really mastered quilting as I was more interested in color and shape than texture. My quilts turned into art quilts and then art embroidery, which I have shown in exhibitions and galleries all over the world. Eventually I decided to dye my own fabrics and embroidery threads – I couldn't afford chemical dyes so I used plant dyes from my garden and hedgerows. I dyed far too much, so sold it online. A friend suggested that I try dyeing yarn, which proved very successful, so I sold that online too. It quickly became a full-time business and The Natural Dye Studio (NDS) was born.

I have been crocheting for as long as I can remember, but I didn't really take it seriously until I was running NDS, as I needed crochet patterns as support to sell my yarn. But now it has come full circle: after many successful years of business I have stopped dyeing so that I can return to my first love – working with yarn and crocheting.

My inspiration comes from so many different places that it is difficult to pinpoint a single inspiration for each afghan. Every afghan has several ingredients; most are based on my love of textiles and my family roots, but they also normally have some personal relevance to me, such as places I've visited, experiences I have had, the place I live and my family. I normally start by playing with yarn and experimenting with colors and shapes. I'm fascinated with geometry and exploring the way shapes fit together. The inspirations kick in when I've finished a few swatches and decided on an arrangement I like – it influences and helps me decide how I want to arrange the colors. I design as I make, so the afghans start off as a sketch on graph paper, which I edit as I go to come up with the final design. I often end up unpicking whole sections of an afghan because it doesn't quite work.

The yarn itself also has an influence on my designs. I love natural fibres and the way they feel in my hands. Each has its own character, from luxury shiny soft silk to the more rustic wool yarns – I enjoy using them all. I find that many of today's designs don't focus on the yarn type: they are more focused on color and budget than the character of the yarn. I'd like to encourage you to try a range of yarns, even if you can only afford one luxury skein – this is enough to build a whole color collection around. I prefer to use fingering (4-ply) yarn as it means I can make a much more detailed design than when using an 8-ply (DK) or thicker yarn – I can use a greater number of colors in an equivalent space. I try to use as many colors as possible as I like the depth of detail and interest they create. This means my afghans have a lot of ends, so it is essential that I sew the ends in as I go. Sewing ends in is part of my process – I find it like meditation because, as it doesn't involve making any design decisions, it is repetitive and soothing. It also serves the practical purpose of making me hold my hand in an alternative position to the crochet hold, which means I don't put too much stress on my crocheting hand position.

I have several pieces of advice for making the afghans in this book: the first is to consider them an adventure. It is almost impossible to create an exact copy of my afghans – instead, you will create a unique version of your own. So be confident with your color choices. If you are anxious, follow the color wheels as closely as possible, but don't stress about doing it wrong. Also remember that each motif is just a small piece of a jigsaw – if you get one wrong the first time, just try it again. You have only to worry about a small piece to re-make, rather than the work as a whole. If your afghan ends up slightly different to the pattern, that's fine, just as long as you are happy with it. Also, don't worry about time scale: it doesn't matter if it takes you two years to make an afghan, so long as when you have finished you can sit back and enjoy your own achievement at creating a masterpiece. And finally, my most important piece of advice: have fun and enjoy!

Color

Each afghan in the book is made with a collection of rainbow colors. My rainbow color collections are based on The Natural Dye Studio (NDS) colors that I have always used – they aren't the traditional rainbow, as the range of colors that can be created with natural dyes is restricted by the dyes plants can create, and is lacking several colors, such as red. The natural dye colors are subtle, unsaturated shades.

The NDS rainbow

Base your color collections around the NDS rainbow...

Gold   **Green**   **Azure**   **Indigo**   **Violet**   **Rose**   **Orange**

Using a color wheel

I would advise that you use a set of natural colors as a starting point for your collection, but if you're a fan of bright, bold color there is no need to restrict yourself – it's also very likely that you'll already have a few odds and ends in your stash. With this in mind, I have extended the rainbow to form a color wheel, left, adding in colors to create a smooth transition. I find a color wheel useful for seeing the interaction between colors when planning a design and selecting colors. Many companies sell collections of mini skeins of yarn, which can be useful as a starting point. Arrange your skeins or balls of wool in a similar order to see how the colors interact and to check which colors you are missing.

I only use solid or semi-solid colors, as I find that variegated yarn can 'pool' and give the crochet an uneven finish. If you want to use variegated yarns, make sure you choose skeins that have very close colors.

Color density

The afghans in this book are made with combinations of yarns that have a similar depth of color, and so blend well together. If you wish to make any of your own variations, you will need to bear this in mind. I would advise that you do not mix dark and pale colors together in the same afghan – try to use the same color density throughout an afghan. When choosing color, the best way to check if a color is too dark or too pale is to put all the colors together and squint at them – when your eyes aren't focused on any one particular color it should be easy to see the ones that are too light or too dark.

However, these are guidelines, and if you have favourite yarns or color combinations, don't be afraid to try them. Why not crochet a few simple motifs and join them, to see how the colors really look when side by side?

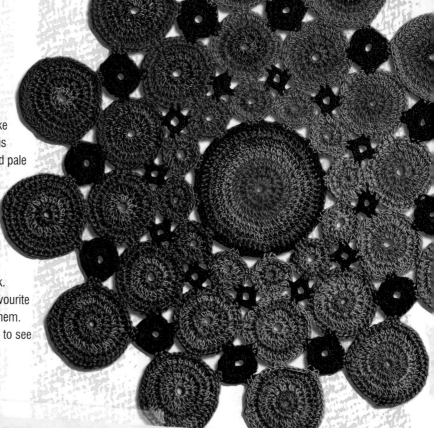

My color collection

The following chart is arranged in rainbow order and is made of swatches of all the colors and their names used in the book. Some of the colors, such as moss, are only used for one afghan, while others, such as rose, are used for most of the afghans.

Gold   Lime   Apple   Green   Moss   Jade   Azure

Cobalt   Indigo   Dark indigo   Heather   Lavender   Violet   Currant

Lilac   Rose   Soft red   Scarlet   Orange   Nutmeg

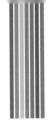

Equipment

Yarn

Rather than prescribe individual yarns for each afghan, I recommend that you make them as scrap afghans. Even when The Natural Dye Studio (NDS) was running, I never made an afghan using yarns from the same dye lot – in part this was because taking 2kg out of the NDS stock at any one time wasn't feasible – but instead I took single skeins of colors that I liked then combined them for my afghans. I love the blend of colors and textures that different dye lots and yarn types give to an afghan.

So I recommend you build up color collections – start with the existing yarns in your stash then add to them (that is, unless you have enough stash for a whole afghan). You can either choose a single yarn type from one brand or buy lots of different yarns from different places. The recommended yarn brands given are all yarns I have tested and used together; some have a huge range of colors and it should be possible to build a whole color collection of the same yarn if you decide to stick to one brand. I have chosen a range of brands that should accommodate most budgets and that are readily available worldwide. I have also listed several luxury independent brands mainly available in the UK, in case you are interested in sourcing these.

I exclusively use natural fibres for my afghans; I'm a self-confessed yarn snob and my favourite yarns are wool, wool/silk, alpaca and alpaca/silk. I live in an area where sheep farming is one of the main industries so I feel it's important to support my local farming community. Natural-fibre yarns have a gorgeous, almost life-like quality. Different sheep breeds all have their own individual character, and the depth of color and texture of their wool is rarely found in synthetic yarn. I firmly believe that if you are going to spend a long time making an heirloom afghan then it deserves to be made with the best yarn you can afford.

Superwash wools are available – these can be put in the washing machine and will not felt – however, I prefer non-superwash as they haven't been through so many processes. Always wash a test swatch before you machine-wash a yarn. I prefer not to use cotton as most cotton yarns have been through a lot of chemical processes and aren't very environmentally friendly. If you would like to use cotton, try to buy organic cotton as it is processed in an environmentally friendly way. Budget is a concern for many people, so do remember that you can use any yarn of the right weight, but you might want to do some test swatching first to check that the yarns work well together.

Recommended yarns

I have tested the following yarns and manufacturers together; they are all roughly the same weight and will work well in the same afghan.

My recommended fingering (4-ply) weight yarns are all 437yd (400m) per 100g. Use with a crochet hook in sizes 3, 3.25 or 3.5mm (US C/2, D/3 or E/4)

My recommended DK (8-ply) or sport yarns are 273yd (240–250m) per 100g. Use with a crochet hook in sizes 4 or 4.5mm (US G/6 or 7)

Worldwide brands:

Drops
- Alpaca (100% alpaca)
- Alpaca/Silk (70% alpaca/30% silk)
- Fabel (75% wool/25% polyester)

Fyberspates
- Vivacious 4-ply (100% merino wool)
- Scrumptious 4-ply (45% silk/ 55% merino wool)

Cascade
- 220 Fingering (100% Peruvian highland wool)
- Heritage Silk (85% merino wool/15% silk)

Knit Picks
- Palette yarn (100% Peruvian highland wool)

Madelinetosh
- Tosh Merino Light (100% merino wool)

UK independent dyers/spinners:

Skein Queen
- Selkino (70% merino wool/ 30% silk)
- Lustrous (50% merino wool/ 50% silk)

John Arbon Textiles
- Exmoor Sock (85% Exmoor Bluefaced wool/15% nylon)
- Knit by Numbers 4-ply (100% merino wool)
- Harvest Hues (65% Falklands merino wool/35% Zwartbles wool)

Easyknits
- Splendour (55% Bluefaced Leicester wool/45% silk)

The Little Grey Sheep
- Stein 4-ply (100% Gotland, Shetland and merino wool)

Worldwide brands:

Cascade
- 220 Sport (100% Peruvian highland wool)

Fyberspates
- Vivacious DK (100% merino wool)

Yarn Stories
- Merino DK (100% merino wool)
- Merino/Alpaca DK (70% wool/30% alpaca)

Knit Picks
- Wool of the Andes Sport (100% Peruvian highland wool)

UK independent dyers/spinners:

John Arbon Textiles
- Knit by Numbers DK (100% merino wool)
- Viola (100% merino wool)

Crochet hooks

When making an afghan it is important to choose the right hook, not only for the weight of the yarn, but also for the position of your hand. Afghans take many hours of crocheting, which can cause hand and wrist pain, so you need to choose a hook that is comfortable to use. I prefer a metal hook, but metal can be cold, so I use a metal hook with a plastic handle. There are a number of ergonomic hooks on the market, which can make a huge difference to comfort. They help position your hand so as to minimize pain; however, there are several ways to hold a hook. I hold mine like a pencil and have found most of the ergonomic hooks position my hand in an uncomfortable way. So always test a hook before you buy. If you suffer from painful hands it is worth swapping hooks throughout a project – and sometimes working at a slightly different angle helps. For a list of crochet hook size conversions, see page 128.

Sewing-in needles

Rather than blunt darning needles I use chenille sewing needles for sewing in my yarn ends – the point is sharper and the eye smaller. Ensure that the eye is not too small or it will be difficult to thread.

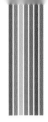

Techniques

Stitches

All of my afghans use only basic stitches – they are designed to showcase color and shape, not complex stitches and difficult techniques. The terms given throughout this book are US crochet terms; for a list of US and UK conversions, see page 128.

Gauge

Although each pattern gives a finished motif size, achieving this exact size isn't vitally important – it doesn't actually matter if your finished afghan is a little bit bigger or smaller than mine. However, you will need to make sure your stitches aren't too tight or too loose, and that they are consistent across the whole afghan. If the stitches are too tight the finished effect will be quite rigid and unpliable; if the stitches are too loose the afghan will be too floppy.

I use a 3mm (US C/2 or D/3) hook for fingering (4-ply) yarn and a 4mm (US G/6) hook for DK (8-ply) yarn. I crochet with a fairly loose gauge so you might need to go up a hook size or two to get a similar gauge. Those new to crochet are often anxious and so their stitches can be quite tight – experiment with different sized hooks until you find the right one.

Joining motifs

All the afghans are composed entirely of finished motifs, joined together. I join them as I go, rather than making them all first and joining them at the end. I join them with the tail end of the last round of each motif – this ensures they are joined with the same color, which blends into the overall color of the afghan. Joining them as you finish them also makes it easier to follow the step-by-step charts.

You can either crochet or sew the motifs together – I use a slip stitch. Hold two motifs together face to face, with the motif you are working on, on top. Slip stitch or sew into the corresponding gaps on each side of the motif. When joining into a three, four or five-sided corner, make sure you slip stitch or sew one stitch in to the opposite corner to close up the gap created by the curved corners. If the afghan has fillers you will need to leave a gap and should only join the sides.

Sewing in ends

Do not wait to start sewing in your ends until the afghan is complete or you will end up spending days and days sewing. I sew mine every day before I start to crochet – weaving in the ends becomes part of the process and if you only have a few motifs, it won't take long. I prefer to sew in all my ends, as it firms up the motifs and seams, making them more solid. To ensure the ends don't pop out, sew the end from the back under the stitches in one direction, then turn the needle round and sew back through the stitches you have just sewn. This may leave a little bump but it will smooth out and become unnoticeable when the afghan is washed.

Outer border

A lot of my afghans don't have borders as I like to see the effect of the color changes all the way to the edges of the afghan. The bordered afghans are normally bordered with two rows of either single crochet or half double crochet. To create this effect you need to crochet into the gaps between the stitches. When you reach a corner, crochet two stitches with two chains between them – this defines the corners, rather than making them curl. For an inward facing corner, miss the last stitch of each side of the motif – this will make the inward corners tighter rather than gape.

Blocking

I normally don't block my motifs while making an afghan, as the motifs are joined as they are made. The motif sizes given in the patterns are for washed and dried motifs: make a test motif, then wet it and dry it flat to give you an idea of the finished size.

I don't block my afghans as they are usually far too large, but I always wash them. Washing them neatens the stitches and helps them lie correctly. I wet them in the sink and then use a top-loading old-fashioned spin drier to spin as much of the water out as possible. If you don't have a drier you can spin the afghan in your washing machine on the shortest spin setting – this should be fine for cotton, silk and superwash yarns; you will need to check the yarn manufacturer's instructions on how to wash and spin acrylic. Before you spin the whole afghan, I suggest you test a swatch of yarn in your normal wash. Spread out the washed afghans flat in the sun or dry them indoors on the floor. I purchased two old bed spreads from the local thrift store – I lay them on the floor then spread the afghan out on top.

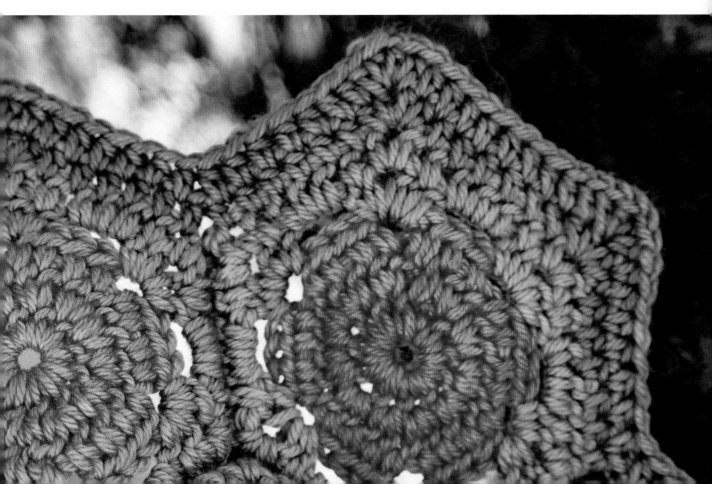

The Projects

How to use this book

Although some of my designs look quite complex, they are built up of lots of simple motifs and are actually deceptively easy. In the past, crochet has been thought of as something you do with scraps of yarn left over from knitting projects, and that granny squares are the only motif out there... but things are changing! There are now many fabulous crochet designers, which has resulted in crochet workshops popping up in shops all over the place and more and more new crocheters learning the basics online. This has led to a huge number of new crocheters, many of whom struggle to read the traditionally written patterns. I want to encourage them to have the confidence to explore the world of crochet so I have developed a simple pattern format. I write them slightly longer hand than you might be used to seeing: I want them to be logical and simple to understand, so that everyone can have the confidence to follow them, including beginners.

Creating each project

Every project contains the following: the finished size of the afghan, hook size and yarn type needed, along with a list of recommended yarns. I've also included a color illustration of the whole afghan, so that you can see at a glance how the whole thing is constructed. Every afghan is made up of a number of simple motifs. For each motif I have given the pattern both written out and as a stitch chart, alongside a photograph of the motif referred to. I've given an example motif stitch chart with instructions and key, right.

   Once you have mastered the motifs you will need to refer to the layout key to work out how many of each you need to make. The key contains the color of each round of the motif, plus the number of motifs you need to crochet in that specific color order. The motif numbers given in the key correspond to the step-by-step instructions given for each afghan, which will help you piece together your afghan a step at a time. There are plenty of gorgeous photographs of the afghans given, to show you how the finished item will look. Finally, each project comes with two color variations – try them if you're feeling more adventurous.

Reading a crochet chart

A stitch chart is just a drawing of a motif in which the symbols are laid out like a map. Each stitch has its own symbol. The symbols are universal, unlike the crochet terms: so as long as you understand what the symbol means you don't need to know the name of the stitch, just the method of crocheting it. See the stitch guide key, right.

I write the pattern in full for one side of each round, always starting in the corner and working across to the next corner. In most cases, this pattern is then simply repeated across the remaining sides; for a square, you need to crochet the pattern three further times, a hexagon five further times and a triangle two further times, until you get back to the starting corner.

The stitch chart

Given right is a hexagon motif chart with the first side of round 5 colored dark green. I have given the corresponding instructions below for this final round of stitches – both for the stitches shown in dark green and the rest of the round – this should help you visualize how the pattern works.

As you can see, each new round of a motif starts with a set of chain stitches. These stitches are the equivalent of the stitch they are replacing, for example, 2 chains are the same height as 1 hdc stitch and 3 chains are the same height as 1 dc. So here the pattern reads '2 ch (counts as 1 hdc)'. The chain sts are only used for the first side of the motif – all of the other sides will start with the actual stitch.

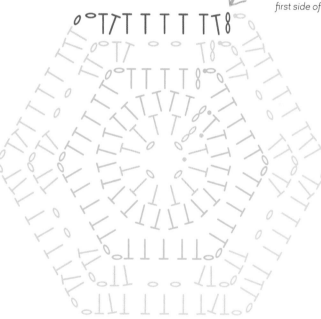

Start here with two chains, the equivalent of 1 hdc, then work to the left to create the first side of the hexagon.

Please note!

All my motifs are made by crocheting into the gaps between stitches rather than crocheting into the actual stitch itself.

Round 5, shown in dark green: 2 ch (counts as 1 hdc), 1 hdc in same space, *1 hdc in next gap, 3 hdc in the 2-ch space, 1 hdc in next gap, (2 hdc, 2 ch**, 2 hdc) in the 2-ch corner space*.

The rest of round 5: repeat from * to * 5 more times ending last repeat at **. Join to the 2nd st of original 2-ch with a sl st. Fasten off.

Crop Circles

I am fascinated by circles and love creating designs with them. Crop circles are a good example of their use, and a great source of inspiration – whether you believe they are man-made or made by unknown entities. I prefer the older, simpler designs; a lot of the more recent designs are very complex. Farmers must hate the destruction of their crops, but the dedication of their makers has to be admired – it must be difficult constructing them and ensuring they are perfect under cover of night. The yellow-gold background in this afghan represents the color of the cornfields in which the crop circles appear.

Afghan size
71 x 75in (180.5 x 190.5cm)

Hook size
3 or 3.25mm (US C/2 or D/3)

Yarn type
Fingering (4-ply) yarn:
  394yd (360m) per 100g

Yarn notes
I made this afghan with oddments of yarn left over from other projects. If you prefer to buy new yarn, consider choosing the yarn brands below. You do not need to use the same dye lots.

Color palette

This project has one basic square motif that is created in six color variations. Refer to the layout key on page 23.

| Gold: 1500g | Orange: 100g | Soft red: 100g | Rose: 100g | Lilac: 100g |
| Currant: 100g | Indigo: 100g | Azure: 200g | Green: 100g | Lime: 100g |

Worldwide brands:
Drops: Alpaca, Alpaca/Silk
Fyberspates: Vivacious 4-ply
Cascade: 220 Fingering, Heritage Silk
Knit Picks: Palette yarn

UK independent dyers and spinners:
Skein Queen: Selkino, Lustrous
John Arbon Textiles: Exmoor Sock,
Knit by Numbers 4-ply
Easyknits: Splendour
The Little Grey Sheep: Stein 4-ply

Construction

JOINING: The finished squares are slip stitched or crocheted together along each side. Crochet into the corresponding gaps between the stitches on each side of each motif.

BORDER: Work two rows of single crochet.

Color chart

This chart is designed to give you an overall look at how this afghan is composed and how the colors interact with each other; there is further detail on the afghan's motif arrangement in the step-by-step section (pages 24–25). The most prominent color here is yellow-gold but you don't need to use the same colors as I have. There are two other color variation charts for inspiration on pages 26–27.

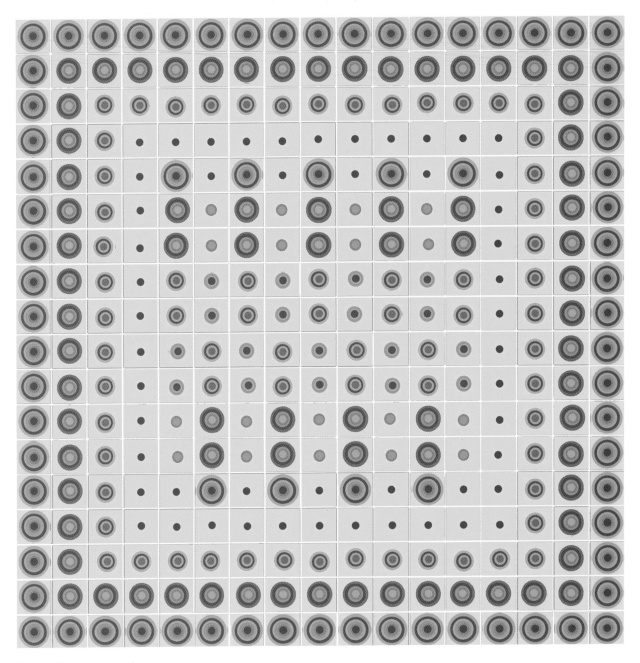

The motif arrangement

Square motif
4 x 4in (10 x 10cm)

Using color 1, make a 5-ch foundation chain and join in a ring with a sl st.

Round 1: 2 ch (counts as 1 hdc), 9 hdc in the foundation ring. Join to the 2nd st of original 2-ch with a sl st (10 hdc). Fasten off.

Round 2: in this and all following rounds, work in the gaps between sts in previous round. Join color 2 in any gap, 2 ch (counts as 1 hdc), 1 hdc in same gap, *2 hdc in next gap*. Repeat from * to * 8 times. Join to the 2nd st of original 2-ch with a sl st (20 hdc). Fasten off.

Round 3: join color 3 in any gap, 2 ch (counts as 1 hdc), 1 hdc in same gap, 1 hdc in next gap, *2 hdc in next gap, 1 hdc in next gap*. Repeat from * to * 8 times. Join to the 2nd st of original 2-ch with a sl st (30 hdc). Fasten off.

Round 4: join color 4 in any gap, 2 ch (counts as 1 hdc), 1 hdc in the same gap, 1 hdc in the next 2 gaps, *2 hdc in next gap, 1 hdc in next 2 gaps, *. Repeat from * to * 8 times. Join to the 2nd st of original 2-ch with a sl st (40 hdc). Fasten off.

Round 5: join color 5 in any gap, 2 ch (counts as 1 hdc), 1 hdc in same gap, 1 hdc in the next 3 gaps, *2 hdc in next gap, 1 hdc in next 3 gaps*. Repeat from * to * 8 times. Join to the 2nd st of original 2-ch with a sl st (50 hdc). Fasten off.

Round 6: join color 6 in any gap, 2 ch (counts as 1 hdc), 1 hdc in same gap, 1 hdc in the next 4 gaps, *2 hdc in next gap, 1 hdc in next 4 gaps*. Repeat from * to * 8 times. Join to the 2nd st of original 2-ch with a sl st (60 hdc). Fasten off.

Round 7: join color 7 in any gap, 4 ch (counts as 1 tr), 1 tr in same gap (this forms the end of a corner), *1 tr in the next gap, 1 dc in the next 2 gaps, 1 hdc in the next 2 gaps, 1 sc in the next 4 gaps, 1 hdc in the next 2 gaps, 1 dc in the next 2 gaps, 1 tr in the next gap, (2 tr, 2 ch**, 2 tr) in the next gap (this forms the corner)*. Repeat from * to * 3 times ending last repeat at **. Join to the 4th st of original 4-ch with a sl st.

Round 8: 1 ch (counts as 1sc) in the 2-ch corner space, *1 sc in the next 17 gaps, (1 sc, 2 ch**, 1 sc) in the 2-ch corner space*. Repeat from * to * 3 times, ending last repeat at **. Join to the original 1-ch with a sl st. Fasten off.

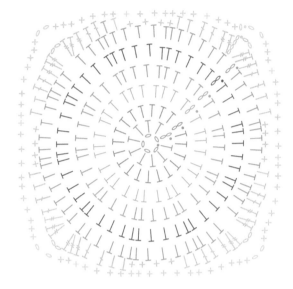

The motif stitch diagram

The layout key

Motif	Round 1	Round 2	Round 3	Round 4	Round 5	Round 6	Rounds 7 & 8
1: make 51	Orange, soft red, rose, lilac, currant, indigo, azure, green or lime	Gold	Gold	Gold	Gold	Gold	Gold
2: make 18	Orange, soft red, rose, lilac, currant, indigo, azure, green or lime	Orange, soft red, rose, lilac, currant, indigo, azure, green or lime	Gold	Gold	Gold	Gold	Gold
3: make 18	Orange, soft red, rose, lilac, currant, indigo, azure, green or lime	Orange, soft red, rose, lilac, currant, indigo, azure, green or lime	Orange, soft red, rose, lilac, currant, indigo, azure, green or lime	Gold	Gold	Gold	Gold
4: make 68	Orange, soft red, rose, lilac, currant, indigo, azure, green or lime	Orange, soft red, rose, lilac, currant, indigo, azure, green or lime	Orange, soft red, rose, lilac, currant, indigo, azure, green or lime	Orange, soft red, rose, lilac, currant, indigo, azure, green or lime	Gold	Gold	Gold
5: make 76	Orange, soft red, rose, lilac, currant, indigo, azure, green or lime	Orange, soft red, rose, lilac, currant, indigo, azure, green or lime	Orange, soft red, rose, lilac, currant, indigo, azure, green or lime	Orange, soft red, rose, lilac, currant, indigo, azure, green or lime	Orange, soft red, rose, lilac, currant, indigo, azure, green or lime	Gold	Gold
6: make 75	Orange, soft red, rose, lilac, currant, indigo, azure, green or lime	Orange, soft red, rose, lilac, currant, indigo, azure, green or lime	Orange, soft red, rose, lilac, currant, indigo, azure, green or lime	Orange, soft red, rose, lilac, currant, indigo, azure, green or lime	Orange, soft red, rose, lilac, currant, indigo, azure, green or lime	Orange, soft red, rose, lilac, currant, indigo, azure, green or lime	Gold

Making Crop Circles

1 Take one Motif 1 block, two Motif 2 blocks, two Motif 3 blocks, two Motif 4 blocks, two Motif 5 blocks and one Motif 6 block. Attach them together with slip stitch in the order shown to create the center column.

2 Take two Motif 1 blocks, four Motif 2 blocks, four Motif 3 blocks, four Motif 4 blocks, four Motif 5 blocks and two Motif 6 blocks. Taking one side at a time, add a column either side of the first column with slip stitch.

3 Take six Motif 1 blocks, twelve Motif 2 blocks, twelve Motif 3 blocks, twelve Motif 4 blocks, twelve Motif 5 blocks and six Motif 6 blocks. As in step 2, work a column at a time as shown, attaching the blocks with slip stitch.

Step 1

6
5
5
4
4
3
3
2
2
1

Step 2

1	6	1
2	5	2
2	5	2
3	4	3
3	4	3
4	3	4
4	3	4
5	2	5
5	2	5
6	1	6

Step 3

6	1	6	1	6	1	6	1	6
5	2	5	2	5	2	5	2	5
5	2	5	2	5	2	5	2	5
4	3	4	3	4	3	4	3	4
4	3	4	3	4	3	4	3	4
3	4	3	4	3	4	3	4	3
3	4	3	4	3	4	3	4	3
2	5	2	5	2	5	2	5	2
2	5	2	5	2	5	2	5	2
1	6	1	6	1	6	1	6	1

4 The center block is now complete and you can start adding the next motifs in rounds, working around the afghan as you add them. Take forty-two Motif 1 blocks and slip stitch them in place to create the first border.

5 Take fifty Motif 4 blocks and slip stitch them in place to create the second border.

6 Take fifty-eight Motif 5 blocks and slip stitch them in place to create the third border.

7 Take sixty-six Motif 6 blocks and slip stitch them in place to create the fourth border.

8 Complete the afghan with a 2 sc border.

6	6	6	6	6	6	6	6	6	6	6	6	6	6	6	6	6	6
6	5	5	5	5	5	5	5	5	5	5	5	5	5	5	5	5	6
6	5	4	4	4	4	4	4	4	4	4	4	4	4	4	4	5	6
6	5	4	1	1	1	1	1	1	1	1	1	1	1	1	4	5	6
6	5	4	1	6	1	6	1	6	1	6	1	6	1	1	4	5	6
6	5	4	1	5	2	5	2	5	2	5	2	5	2	1	4	5	6
6	5	4	1	5	2	5	2	5	2	5	2	5	2	1	4	5	6
6	5	4	1	4	3	4	3	4	3	4	3	4	3	1	4	5	6
6	5	4	1	4	3	4	3	4	3	4	3	4	3	1	4	5	6
6	5	4	1	3	4	3	4	3	4	3	4	3	4	1	4	5	6
6	5	4	1	3	4	3	4	3	4	3	4	3	4	1	4	5	6
6	5	4	1	2	5	2	5	2	5	2	5	2	5	1	4	5	6
6	5	4	1	2	5	2	5	2	5	2	5	2	5	1	4	5	6
6	5	4	1	1	6	1	6	1	6	1	6	1	6	1	4	5	6
6	5	4	1	1	1	1	1	1	1	1	1	1	1	1	4	5	6
6	5	4	4	4	4	4	4	4	4	4	4	4	4	4	4	5	6
6	5	5	5	5	5	5	5	5	5	5	5	5	5	5	5	5	6
6	6	6	6	6	6	6	6	6	6	6	6	6	6	6	6	6	6

Steps 4–7

Color variations

For this variation I changed the 'background' color to a deep
purple, and used lots of gorgeous berry and blue tones.

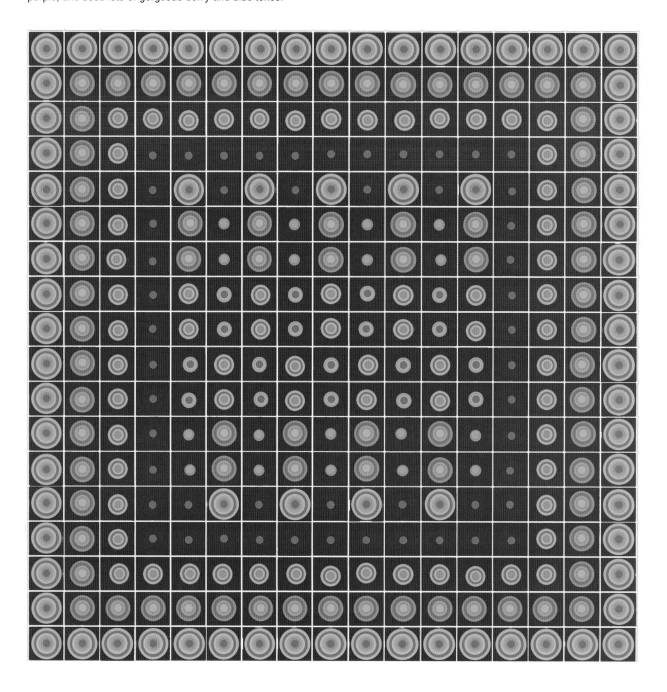

Color variations

For this variation I changed the 'background' color to a bright
lime green, and used lots of fresh, vibrant colors.

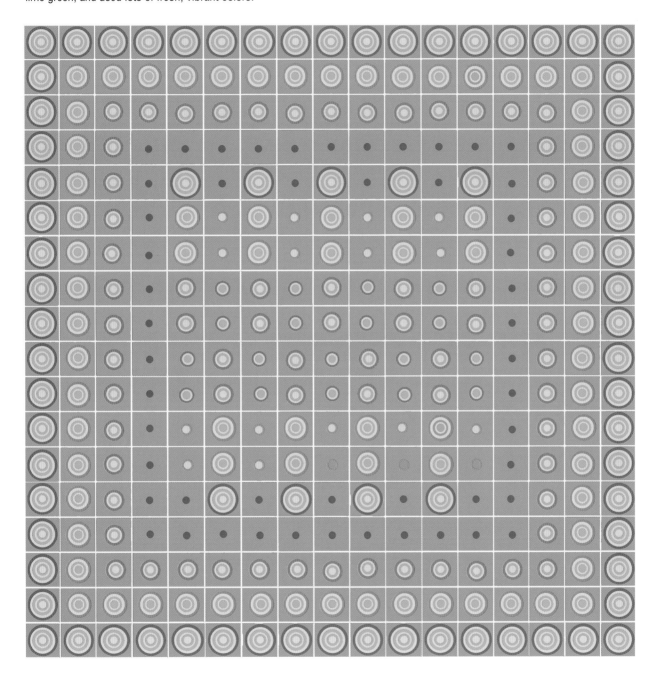

Solstice

Solstice is the sister afghan to Crop Circles because I wanted to develop the design into a rainbow afghan. It is named Solstice in honour of the summer solstice celebrated at Stonehenge in Wiltshire, UK. Wiltshire is a county in which a lot of crop circles appear, especially in the areas around ancient monuments like Stonehenge. Every year thousands of colorfully dressed pagans travel to the henge from all over the world – hence the rainbow colors. Incidentally, I'm not one of them, but I love the idea that they are passionate enough to travel so far to see a sunrise.

Afghan size
50 x 56in (127 x 142.25cm)

Hook size
4mm (US G/6)

Yarn type
DK (8-ply) yarn: 263–273yd (240–250m) per 100g

Yarn notes
I made this afghan with oddments of yarn left over from other projects. If you prefer to buy new yarn, consider choosing the yarn brands below. You do not need to use the same dye lots.

Worldwide brands:
Cascade: 220 Sport
Fyberspates: Vivacious DK
Yarn Stories: Merino DK, Merino/Alpaca DK
Knit Picks: Wool of the Andes Sport

UK independent dyers and spinners:
John Arbon Textiles: Knit by Numbers DK

Color palette

The motif pattern used here is exactly the same as the one used for the Crop Circles project, but with a variety of different colors.

Gold: 150g

Orange: 150g

Soft red: 150g

Rose: 150g

Violet: 150g

Heather: 200g

Indigo: 200g

Cobalt: 200g

Azure: 200g

Apple: 200g

Construction

JOINING: The finished squares are slip stitched or crocheted together along each side. Crochet into the corresponding gaps between the stitches on each side of each motif.

FINISHING: Solstice doesn't have edging as I wanted to show off the definition of each square. However, if you prefer to edge your afghan, work two rows of single crochet.

Color chart

This chart is designed to give you an overall look at how this afghan is composed, and how the colors interact with each other; there is further detail on the afghan's motif arrangement in the step-by-step section (page 34). There are two other color variation charts for inspiration on pages 36 and 37.

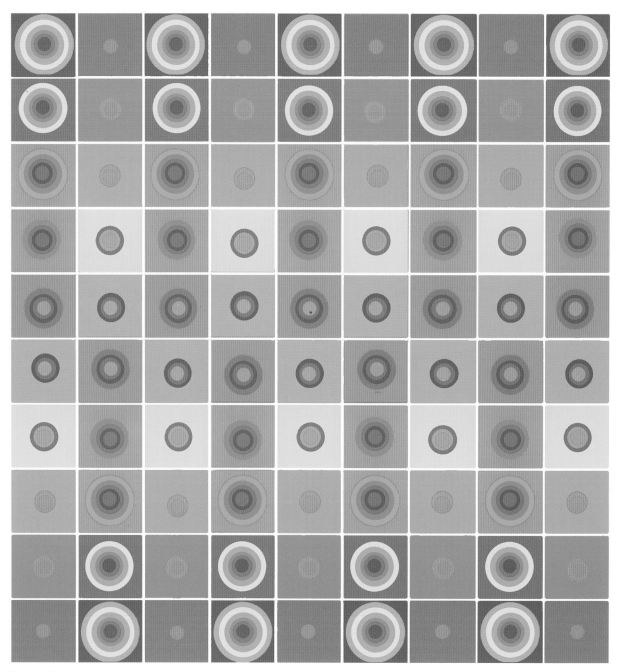

The motif arrangement

Square motif

5¼ x 5¼in (13 x 13cm)

Using color 1, make a 5-ch foundation chain and join in a ring with a sl st.

Round 1: 2 ch (counts as 1 hdc), 9 hdc in the foundation ring. Join to the 2nd st of original 2-ch with a sl st (10 hdc). Fasten off.

Round 2: in this and all following rounds, work in the gaps between sts in previous round. Join color 2 in any gap, 2 ch (counts as 1 hdc), 1 hdc in same gap, *2 hdc in next gap*. Repeat from * to * 8 times. Join to the 2nd st of original 2-ch with a sl st (20 hdc). Fasten off.

Round 3: join color 3 in any gap, 2 ch (counts as 1 hdc), 1 hdc in same gap, 1 hdc in next gap, *2 hdc in next gap, 1 hdc in next gap*. Repeat from * to * 8 times. Join to the 2nd st of original 2-ch with a sl st (30 hdc). Fasten off.

Round 4: join color 4 in any gap, 2 ch (counts as 1 hdc), 1 hdc in the same gap, 1 hdc in the next 2 gaps, *2 hdc in next gap, 1 hdc in next 2 gaps*. Repeat from * to * 8 times. Join to the 2nd st of original 2-ch with a sl st (40 hdc). Fasten off.

Round 5: join color 5 in any gap, 2 ch (counts as 1 hdc), 1 hdc in same gap, 1 hdc in the next 3 gaps, *2 hdc in next gap, 1 hdc in next 3 gaps*. Repeat from * to * 8 times. Join to the 2nd st of original 2-ch with a sl st (50 hdc). Fasten off.

Round 6: join color 6 in any gap, 2 ch (counts as 1 hdc), 1 hdc in same gap, 1 hdc in the next 4 gaps, *2 hdc in next gap, 1 hdc in next 4 gaps*. Repeat from * to * 8 times. Join to the 2nd st of original 2-ch with a sl st (60 hdc). Fasten off.

Round 7: join color 7 in any gap, 4 ch (counts as 1 tr), 1 tr in same gap (this forms the end of a corner), *1 tr in the next gap, 1 dc in the next 2 gaps, 1 hdc in the next 2 gaps, 1 sc in the next 4 gaps, 1 hdc in the next 2 gaps, 1 dc in the next 2 gaps, 1 tr in the next gap, (2 tr, 2 ch**, 2 tr) in the next gap (this forms the corner)*. Repeat from * to * 3 times ending last repeat at **. Join to the 4th st of original 4-ch with a sl st.

Round 8: 1 ch (counts as 1 sc) in the 2-ch corner space, *1 sc in the next 17 gaps, (1 sc, 2 ch**, 1 sc) in the 2-ch corner space*. Repeat from * to * 3 times, ending last repeat at **. Join to the original 1-ch with a sl st. Fasten off.

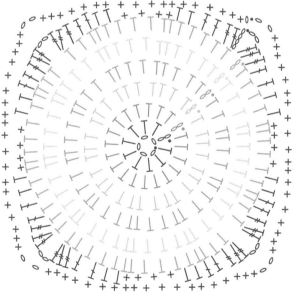

The motif stitch diagram

The layout key

Motif	Round 1	Round 2	Round 3	Round 4	Round 5	Round 6	Rounds 7 & 8
1: make 9	Soft red	Cobalt	Cobalt	Cobalt	Cobalt	Cobalt	Cobalt
2: make 9	Soft red	Rose	Azure	Azure	Azure	Azure	Azure
3: make 9	Rose	Violet	Apple	Apple	Apple	Apple	Apple
4: make 9	Rose	Violet	Heather	Gold	Gold	Gold	Gold
5: make 9	Violet	Heather	Indigo	Orange	Orange	Orange	Orange
6: make 9	Violet	Heather	Indigo	Cobalt	Soft red	Soft red	Soft red
7: make 9	Heather	Indigo	Cobalt	Azure	Rose	Rose	Rose
8: make 9	Heather	Indigo	Cobalt	Azure	Apple	Violet	Violet
9: make 9	Indigo	Cobalt	Azure	Apple	Gold	Heather	Heather
10: make 9	Indigo	Cobalt	Azure	Apple	Gold	Orange	Indigo

Making Solstice

1 Take one of each Motif block. Start with the central column of the afghan and work from the top downwards, joining the blocks together with slip stitch.

2 Take a further two of each Motif block. Add a column at a time either side of the center column, attaching the blocks with slip stitch.

3 Take the remaining six sets of motifs. Continue to join the blocks together with slip stitch, a column at a time as shown, until the afghan is complete.

Step 1 **Step 2** **Step 3**

Color variations

For this variation I arranged the motifs so that the overall rainbow gradation moved diagonally across the afghan.

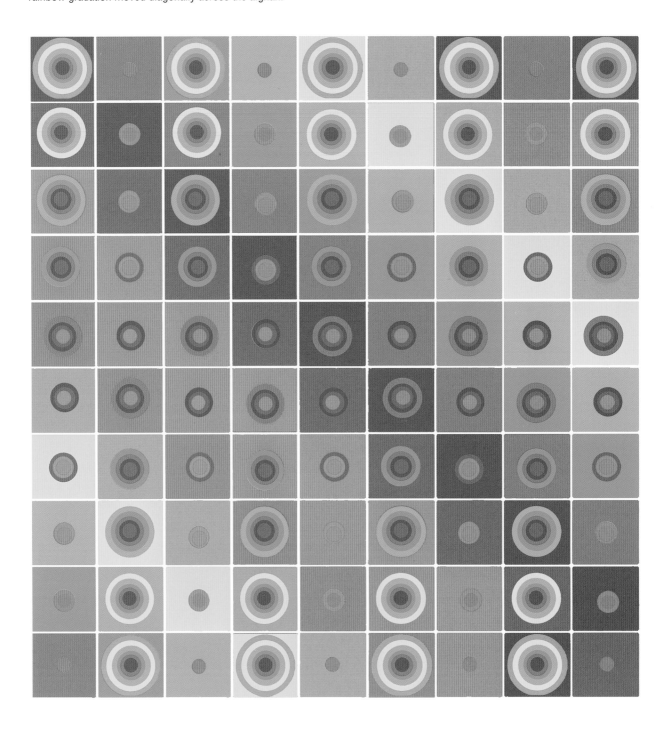

Color variations

For this variation I created a more formalized arrangement of colors,
keeping the focus on the increase and decrease in the size of the circles.

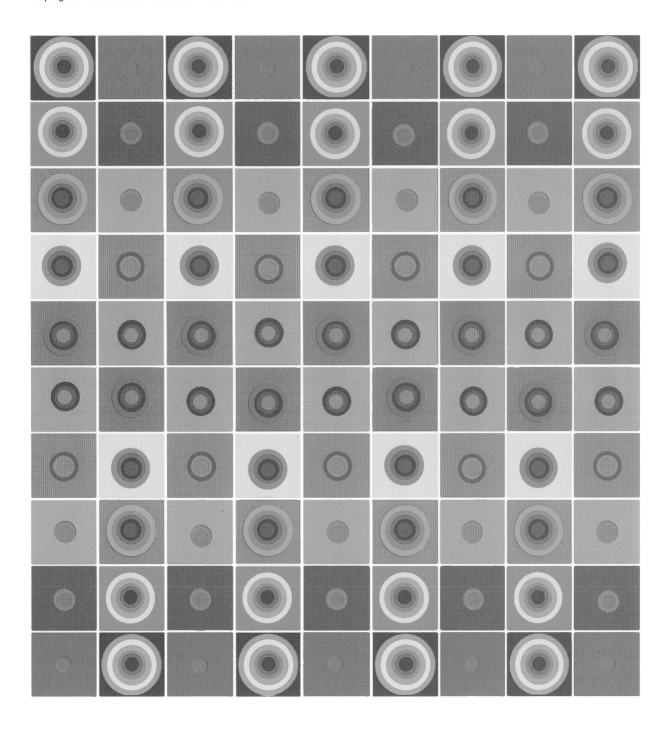

Arabian Nights

I love fairy tales; one of my favourite collections is *One Thousand and One Nights*, commonly known as *Arabian Nights*. The tales were told by Scheherazade to her King and include *Aladdin, Sinbad the Sailor* and *Ali Baba and the Forty Thieves*. This afghan is inspired by design elements from Persian carpets and Aladdin's magic carpet ride. The base color is orange-red as most historic carpets are dyed with madder, which is one of my favourites. The best madder comes from Iran – it's an earthy, rich dye and I always think it smells of the desert.

Afghan size
60 x 65in (150 x 165cm), excluding tassels

Hook size
4mm (US G/6)

Yarn type
DK (8-ply) yarn: 263–273yd (240–250m) per 100g

Yarn notes
I made this afghan with oddments of yarn left over from other projects. If you prefer to buy new yarn, consider choosing the yarn brands below. You do not need to use the same dye lots.

Color palette

You can use up oddments and leftovers from other projects.

Gold: 150g   Orange: 800g   Soft red: 450g   Rose: 100g   Violet: 150g

Cobalt: 150g   Azure: 50g   Apple: 100g   Lime: 250g

Worldwide brands:
Cascade: 220 Sport
Fyberspates: Vivacious DK
Yarn Stories: Merino DK, Merino/Alpaca DK
Knit Picks: Wool of the Andes Sport

UK Independent dyers and spinners:
John Arbon Textiles: Knit by Numbers DK

Construction

The afghan is worked in strips of squares and triangles: start at the top and work downwards. If you are using a collection of different yarns and shades, alternate them for each motif to ensure an even balance.

JOINING: The finished squares are slip stitched or crocheted together along each side. Crochet into the corresponding gaps between the stitches on each side of the motif.

FINISHING: To create a border, work two rows of half double crochet.

Color chart

This chart is designed to give you an overall look at how this afghan is composed, and how the colors interact with each other; there is further detail on the afghan's motif arrangement in the step-by-step section (pages 44–45). There are two other color variation charts for inspiration on pages 48 and 49.

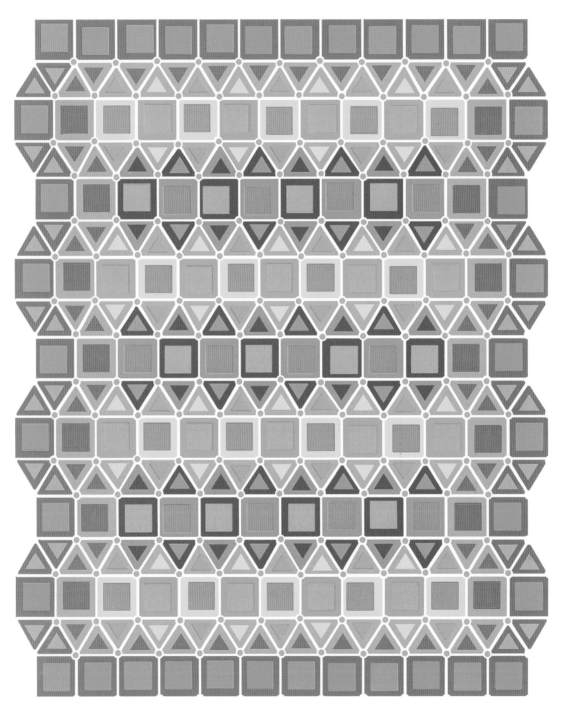

The motif arrangement

Square motif

3½ x 3½in (9 x 9cm)

Using color 1, make a 4-ch foundation chain and join in a ring with a sl st.

Round 1: 2 ch (counts as 1 hdc), 11 hdc in the foundation ring. Join to the 2nd st of original 2-ch with a sl st (12 hdc).

Round 2: in this and all following rounds work into the gaps between sts from the previous round. 2 ch (counts as 1 hdc), 1 hdc in same gap, *2 hdc in next gap*. Repeat from * to * 10 times. Join to the 2nd st of original 2-ch with a sl st (24 hdc).

Round 3: 3 ch (counts as 1 dc) in the first gap, *1 hdc in next gap, 1 sc in the next 3 gaps, 1 hdc in next gap, (1 dc, 2 ch**, 1 dc) in next gap (this is a corner)*. Repeat from * to * 3 times, ending last repeat at **. Join to the 3rd st of original 3-ch with a sl st. Fasten off.

Round 4: join color 2 in any corner space, 2 ch (counts as 1 hdc), 1 hdc in the same corner space, *1 hdc in the next 6 gaps, (2 hdc, 2 ch**, 2 hdc) in corner space*. Repeat from * to * 3 times, ending last repeat at **. Join to the 2nd st of original 2-ch with a sl st.

Round 5: 2 ch (counts as 1 hdc), 1 hdc in same gap (this is easier to do if you position the hook at a slight angle), 1 hdc in the next 9 gaps, (2 hdc, 2 ch**, 2 hdc) in corner space*. Repeat from * to * 3 times, ending last repeat at **. Join to the 2nd st of original 2-ch with a sl st. Fasten off.

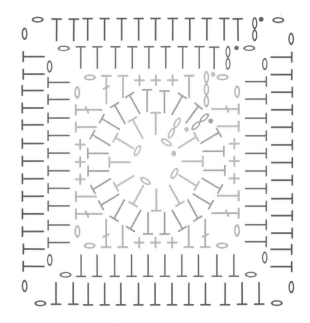

The motif stitch diagram

Triangle motif
3½in (9cm) along each edge

Using color 1, make a 4-ch foundation chain and join in a ring with a sl st.

Round 1: 2 ch (counts as 1 hdc), 3 hdc in foundation ring, 2 ch, *4 hdc in foundation ring, 2 ch*. Repeat from * to * once. Join to the 2nd st of original 2-ch with a sl st.

Round 2: in this and all following rounds work into the gaps between sts from the previous round. 2 ch (counts as 1 hdc), *1 sc in next 3 gaps, (1 hdc, 1 dc, 2 ch, 1 dc**, 1 hdc) in next gap* (this forms the corner). Repeat from * to * twice ending last repeat at **. Join to the 2nd st of original 2-ch with a sl st. Fasten off.

Round 3: join color 2 to a 2-ch corner space, 2 ch (counts as 1 hdc), 1 hdc in same 2-ch corner. *1 hdc in next 6 gaps, (2 hdc, 2 ch**, 2 hdc) in corner space*. Repeat from * to * twice more ending the last repeat at **. Join to the 2nd st of original 2-ch with a sl st.

Round 4: 2 ch (counts as 1 hdc), 1 hdc in same 2-ch corner space (this is easier to do if you position your hook at a slight angle), *1 hdc in next 9 gaps, (2 hdc, 2 ch**, 2 hdc) in next gap (this forms the corner)*. Repeat from * to * twice more ending the last repeat at **. Join to the 2nd st of original 2-ch with a sl st.

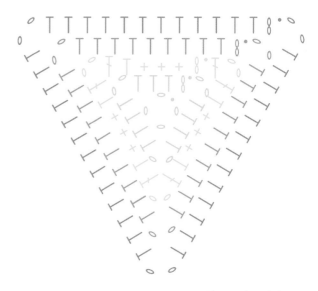

The motif stitch diagram

Filler

Crochet the fillers from the back of the afghan. They will fill the gaps made where two squares and three triangles meet; use the stitches from the existing motifs as the foundation and work inwards. In the example given below, Round 1 is orange and Round 2 is red.

Round 1: join color 1 into a 2-ch corner space, 1 ch (counts as 1 sc), 2 sc into same 2-ch space, *3 sc in next 2-ch space*. Repeat from * to * 3 times. Join to the original 1-ch with a sl st. Fasten off.

Round 2: work inside round 1 into the gaps between the sts. Join color 2 into the first gap after the end of round 1, 1 ch (counts as 1 sc), 1 sc in next gap, miss one gap, *1 sc in next 2 gaps, miss one gap*. Repeat from * to * 3 times. Join to the original 1-ch with a sl st. Fasten off.

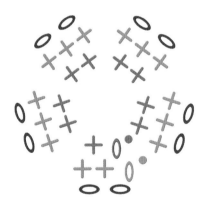

The filler stitch diagram

The layout key

Motif	Rounds 1 & 2	Round 3	Round 4	Round 5
Square motif 1: make 12	Rose	Rose	Cobalt	Cobalt
Square motif 2: make 12	Orange	Orange	Violet	Violet
Triangle motif 3: make 24	Azure	Violet	Violet	
Triangle motif 4: make 24	Violet	Azure	Azure	
Square motif 5: make 18	Rose	Rose	Gold	Gold
Square motif 6: make 18	Orange	Orange	Apple	Apple
Triangle motif 7: make 36	Apple	Orange	Orange	
Triangle motif 8: make 36	Gold	Orange	Orange	
Square motif 9: make 14	Soft red	Soft red	Orange	Orange
Triangle motif 10: make 48	Soft red	Orange	Orange	
Square motif 11: make 19	Cobalt	Cobalt	Soft red	Soft red
Square motif 12: make 19	Apple	Apple	Soft red	Soft red
Triangle motif 13: make 32	Orange	Soft red	Soft red	

Making Arabian Nights

1 Start at the top edge of the afghan and work downwards. Take six square Motif 11 blocks and six square Motif 12 blocks. Begin at the left of the top row and work across, alternating and slip stitching the blocks together.

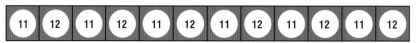

Step 1

2 Take two triangle Motif 13 blocks and ten triangle Motif 10 blocks. Add a row of triangle motifs to the bottom of your first row, using slip stitch.

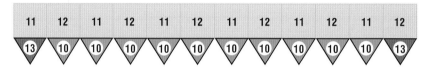

Step 2

3 Take two triangle Motif 13 blocks, two triangle Motif 10 blocks, five triangle Motif 7 blocks and four triangle Motif 8 blocks. Add the next row of triangle motifs, using slip stitch.

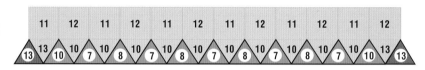

Step 3

4 Add the fillers after every row as you go (shown here in blue between rows 1 and 2), as the spaces are easier to reach, rather than making the whole afghan and adding the fillers later. So add the first set of eleven fillers now, using soft red yarn.

Step 4

5 Take one square Motif 12 block, two square Motif 9 blocks, five square Motif 5 blocks, four square Motif 6 blocks and one square Motif 11 block. Add the next row of square motifs and the next row of twelve fillers, as shown, using orange yarn.

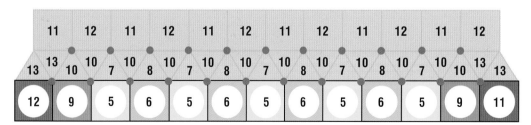

Step 5

6 Continue in this way until you have completed the whole afghan; use orange yarn for all the fillers until you come to the final row – here use soft red yarn again.

Step 6

Tassel motif pattern

Construct twenty-four tassels in total: twelve for each end of the afghan. Join one to the center of each square at each end of the afghan. The tassels are constructed of one triangle and three circles; the triangle is rounds 1, 2 and 3 of the triangle motif and the circles are round 1 of the square motif.

Triangle element of tassel

Using color 1, make a 4-ch foundation chain and join in a ring with a sl st.

Round 1: 2 ch (counts as 1 hdc), 3 hdc in foundation ring, 2 ch, *4 hdc in foundation ring, 2 ch*. Repeat from * to * once. Join to the 2nd st of original 2-ch with a sl st.

Round 2: in this and all following rounds work into the gaps between sts from the previous round. 2 ch (counts as 1 hdc), *1 sc in next 3 gaps, (1 hdc, 1 dc, 2 ch, 1 dc**, 1 hdc) in next gap* (this forms the corner). Repeat from * to * twice ending last repeat at **. Join to the 2nd st of original 2-ch with a sl st. Fasten off.

Round 3: join color 2 to a 2-ch corner space, 2 ch (counts as 1 hdc), 1 hdc in same 2-ch corner. *1 hdc in next 6 gaps, (2 hdc, 2 ch**, 2 hdc) in corner space*. Repeat from * to * twice more ending the last repeat at **. Join to the 2nd st of original 2-ch with a sl st.

Circle element of tassel: make three

Using color 1, make a 4-ch foundation chain and join in a ring with a sl st.

Round 1: 2 ch (counts as 1 hdc), 11 hdc in foundation ring. Join to the 2nd st of original 2-ch with a sl st.

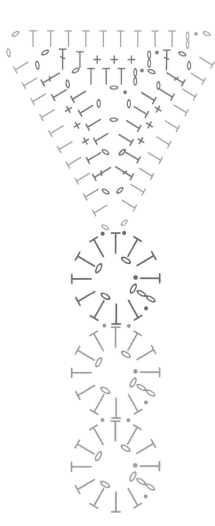

The tassel stitch diagram

Color variations

With a vibrant center and a cool blue-green border, this afghan takes on a very different feel.

Color variations

For this variation I chose soft pinks, purples and blues and
combined them with vivid reds for an elegant finish.

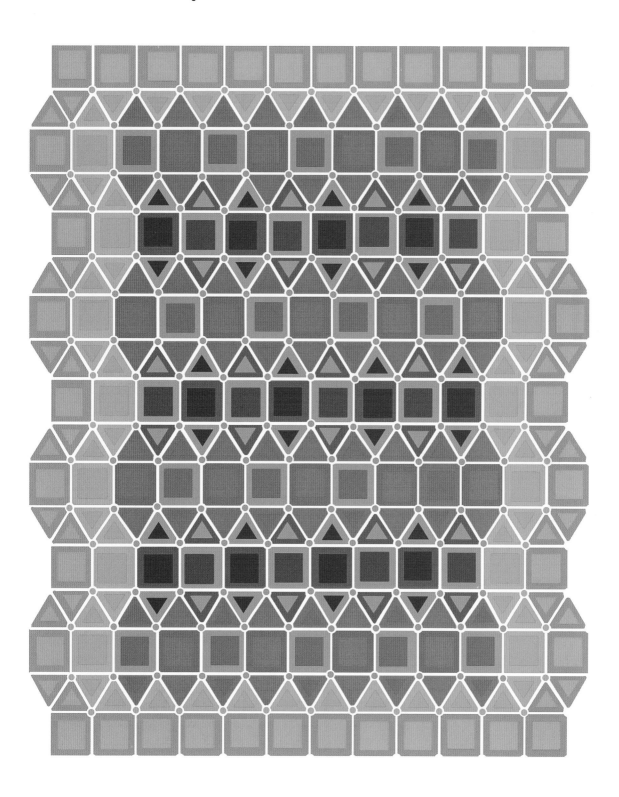

Lilian

This is the sister afghan to Arabian Nights (see pages 38–49). Lilian is the second afghan inspired by design elements from Persian carpets; it is named after a carpet-making area of Iran. My mother was also called Lilian – she loved bright colors, so I chose some of her favourites, including turquoise, jade and pink, for this design.

Afghan size
60 x 65in (150 x 165cm)

Hook size
3 or 3.25mm (US C/2 or D/3)

Yarn type
Fingering (4-ply) yarn:
390yd (360m) per 100g

Yarn notes
I made this afghan with oddments of yarn left over from other projects. If you prefer to buy new yarn, consider choosing the yarn brands below. You do not need to use the same dye lots.

Color palette

You could use oddments and leftovers from other projects.

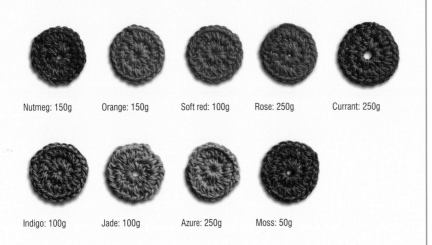

Nutmeg: 150g Orange: 150g Soft red: 100g Rose: 250g Currant: 250g

Indigo: 100g Jade: 100g Azure: 250g Moss: 50g

Worldwide brands:
Drops: Alpaca, Alpaca/Silk
Fyberspates: Vivacious 4-ply
Cascade: 220 Fingering, Heritage Silk
Knit Picks: Palette yarn

UK Independent dyers and spinners:
Skein Queen: Selkino, Lustrous
John Arbon Textiles: Exmoor Sock, Knit by Numbers 4-ply
Easyknits: Splendour
The Little Grey Sheep: Stein 4-ply

Construction

Start at one edge of the afghan and work downwards, adding one row at a time. It is best to add the fillers after every row, as the spaces are easier to reach at this stage, rather than making the whole afghan and adding the fillers later.

JOINING: The finished squares are slip stitched or crocheted together along each side. Crochet into the corresponding gaps between the stitches on each side of the motif.

FINISHING: To create a border, work two rows of half double crochet.

Color chart

This chart is designed to give you an overall look at how this afghan is composed, and how the colors interact with each other; there is further detail on the afghan's motif arrangement in the step-by-step section (pages 58–59). There are two other color variation charts for inspiration on pages 60 and 61.

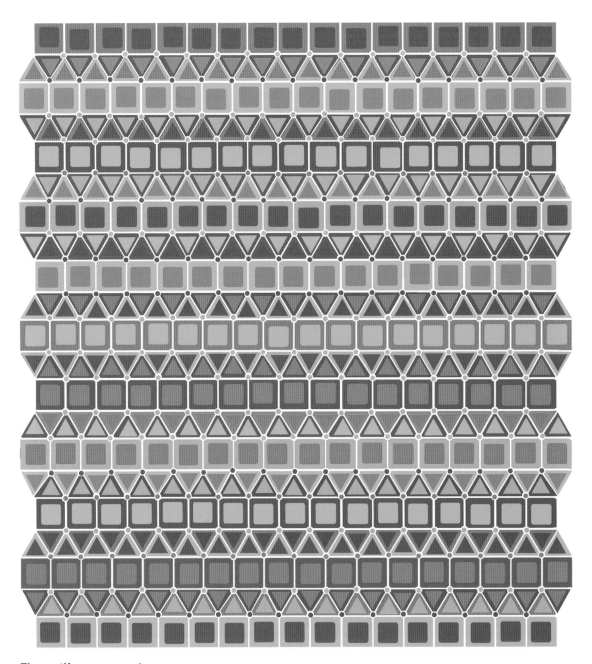

The motif arrangement

Square motif

3 x 3in (7.5 x 7.5cm)

Using color 1, make a 4-ch foundation chain and join in a ring with a sl st.

Round 1: 2 ch (counts as 1 hdc), 11 hdc in the foundation ring. Join to the 2nd st of original 2-ch with a sl st (12 hdc). Fasten off.

Round 2: in this and all following rounds work into the gaps between sts from the previous round. Join color 2 where round 1 completed, 2 ch (counts as 1 hdc),1 hdc in same gap, *2 hdc in next gap*. Repeat from * to * 10 times. Join to the 2nd st of original 2-ch with a sl st (24 hdc). Fasten off.

Round 3: join color 3 where round 2 completed, 3 ch (counts as 1 dc) in the first gap, *1 hdc in next gap, 1 sc in the next 3 gaps, 1 hdc in next gap, (1 dc, 2 ch**, 1 dc) in next gap (this is a corner)*. Repeat from * to * 3 times, ending last repeat at **. Join to the 3rd st of original 3-ch with a sl st. Fasten off.

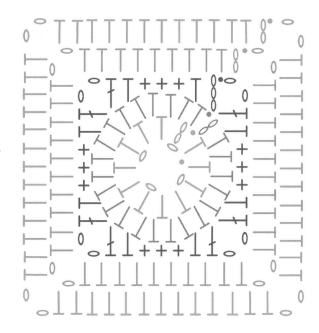

The motif stitch diagram

Round 4: join color 4 in any corner space, 2 ch (counts as 1 hdc), 1 hdc in the same corner space, *1 hdc in the next 6 gaps, (2 hdc, 2 ch**, 2 hdc) in corner space*. Repeat from * to * 3 times, ending last repeat at **. Join to the 2nd st of original 2-ch with a sl st.

Round 5: 2 ch (counts as 1 hdc), 1 hdc in same gap (this is easier to do if you position the hook at a slight angle), 1 hdc in the next 9 gaps, (2 hdc, 2 ch**, 2 hdc) in corner space*. Repeat from * to * 3 times, ending last repeat at **. Join to the 2nd st of original 2-ch with a sl st. Fasten off.

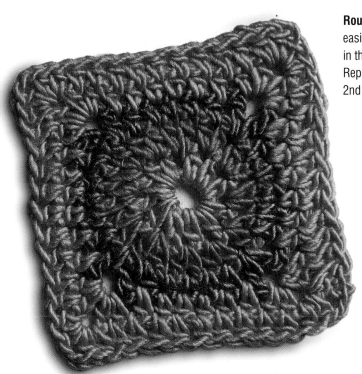

Triangle motif

3in (7.5cm) along each edge

Using color 1, make a 4-ch foundation chain and join in a ring with a sl st.

Round 1: 2 ch (counts as 1 hdc), 3 hdc in foundation ring, 2 ch, *4 hdc in foundation ring, 2 ch*. Repeat from * to * once. Join to the 2nd st of original 2-ch with a sl st. Fasten off.

Round 2: in this and all following rounds work into the gaps between sts from the previous round. Join color 2 to any 2-ch corner space, 2 ch (counts as 1 hdc), *1 sc in next 3 gaps, (1 hdc, 1 dc, 2 ch, 1 dc**, 1 hdc) in next gap* (this forms the corner). Repeat from * to * twice ending last repeat at **. Join to the 2nd st of original 2-ch with a sl st. Fasten off.

Round 3: join color 3 to a 2-ch corner space, 2 ch (counts as 1 hdc), 1 hdc in same 2-ch corner. *1 hdc in next 6 gaps, (2 hdc, 2 ch**, 2 hdc) in corner space*. Repeat from * to * twice more ending the last repeat at **. Join to the 2nd st of original 2-ch with a sl st.

Round 4: 2 ch (counts as 1 hdc), 1 hdc in same 2-ch corner space (this is easier to do if you position your hook at a slight angle), *1 hdc in next 9 gaps, (2 hdc, 2 ch**, 2 hdc) in next gap (this forms the corner)*. Repeat from * to * twice more ending the last repeat at **. Join to the 2nd st of original 2-ch with a sl st. Fasten off.

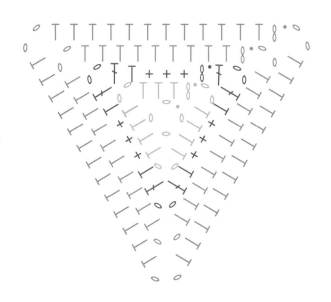

The motif stitch diagram

Filler

Crochet the fillers from the back of the afghan. They will fill the gaps made where two squares and three triangles meet; use the stitches from the existing motifs as the foundation and work inwards. In the example given below, Round 1 is green and Round 2 is blue.

Round 1: join color 1 into a 2-ch corner space, 1 ch (counts as 1 sc), 2 sc into same 2-ch space, *3 sc in next 2-ch space*. Repeat from * to * 3 times. Join to the original 1-ch with a sl st. Fasten off.

Round 2: work inside round 1 into the gaps between the sts. Join color 2 into the first gap after the end of round 1, 1 ch (counts as 1 sc), 1 sc in next gap, miss one gap, *1 sc in next 2 gaps, miss one gap*. Repeat from * to * 3 times. Join to the original 1-ch with a sl st. Fasten off.

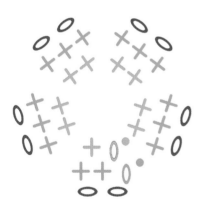

The filler stitch diagram

The layout key

Motif	Round 1	Round 2	Round 3	Round 4	Round 5
Square motif 1: make 17	Rose	Nutmeg	Rose	Rose	Rose
Triangle motif 2: make 17	Nutmeg	Jade	Currant	Currant	
Triangle motif 3: make 18	Rose	Rose	Orange	Orange	
Square motif 4: make 18	Azure	Jade	Indigo	Azure	Azure
Triangle motif 5: make 35	Rose	Orange	Nutmeg	Nutmeg	
Triangle motif 6: make 17	Currant	Currant	Rose	Rose	
Square motif 7: make 34	Azure	Indigo	Jade	Currant	Currant
Triangle motif 8: make 17	Orange	Rose	Soft red	Soft red	
Triangle motif 9: make 36	Indigo	Indigo	Azure	Azure	
Square motif 10: make 18	Rose	Nutmeg	Rose	Orange	Orange
Triangle motif 11: make 36	Indigo	Currant	Currant	Currant	
Triangle motif 12: make 17	Nutmeg	Nutmeg	Soft red	Soft red	
Square motif 13: make 17	Azure	Azure	Jade	Indigo	Azure

Motif	Round 1	Round 2	Round 3	Round 4	Round 5
Triangle motif 14: make 34	Soft red	Rose	Nutmeg	Nutmeg	
Triangle motif 15: make 18	Nutmeg	Currant	Azure	Azure	
Square motif 16: make 18	Indigo	Jade	Rose	Rose	Rose
Triangle motif 17: make 18	Currant	Currant	Orange	Orange	
Square motif 18: make 17	Soft red	Rose	Rose	Currant	Currant
Triangle motif 19: make 17	Rose	Jade	Moss	Moss	
Square motif 20: make 18	Currant	Rose	Rose	Orange	Orange
Triangle motif 21: make 17	Nutmeg	Currant	Rose	Rose	
Triangle motif 22: make 18	Currant	Currant	Azure	Azure	
Square motif 23: make 18	Rose	Rose	Currant	Soft red	Soft red
Triangle motif 24: make 18	Moss	Rose	Currant	Currant	
Triangle motif 25: make 17	Orange	Orange	Rose	Rose	
Square motif 26: make 17	Rose	Currant	Currant	Azure	Azure

Making Lilian

1 Start at the top edge of the afghan and work downwards. Take seventeen square Motif 1 blocks. Begin at the left of the top row and work across, slip stitching the blocks together.

Step 1

2 Take seventeen triangle Motif 2 blocks. Add a row of triangle motifs to the bottom of your first row, using slip stitch.

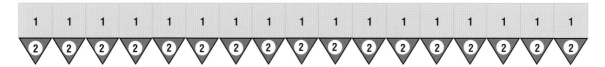

Step 2

3 Take eighteen triangle Motif 3 blocks and add them as the next row, using slip stitch.

4 Add the first set of sixteen fillers, between the Motif 1 squares and Motif 2 triangles; I used azure blue, but use any color you like.

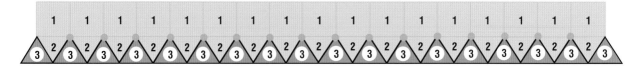

Steps 3 and 4

5 Take eighteen square Motif 4 blocks. Add the next row of square motifs with slip stitch, and the next row of seventeen fillers; I used nutmeg.

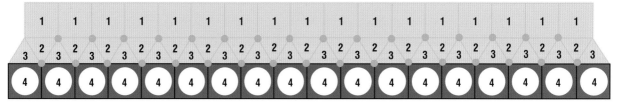

Step 5

6 Continue in this way until you have completed the whole afghan; choose your own colors for fillers: I simply tried to contrast mine with the surrounding motif blocks to ensure they stood out.

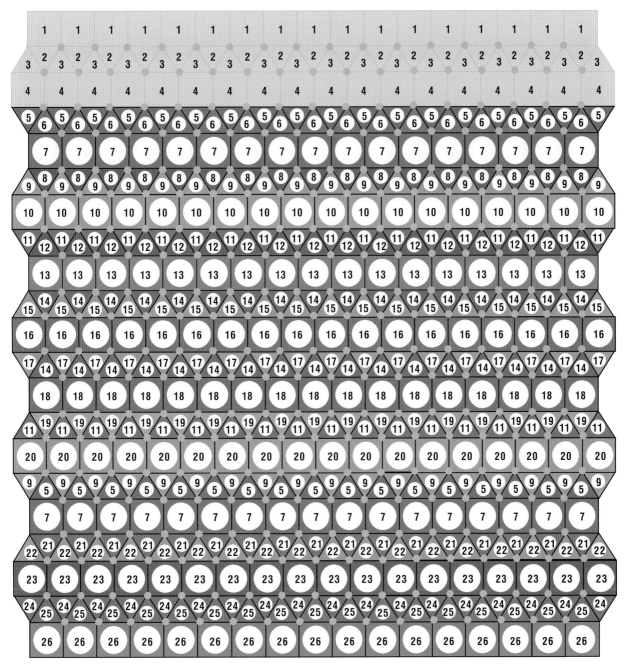

Step 6

Color variations

Choose bright blues, vivid purples and muted greens for a cooler color palette; use
up any odds and ends of yarn within this color range.

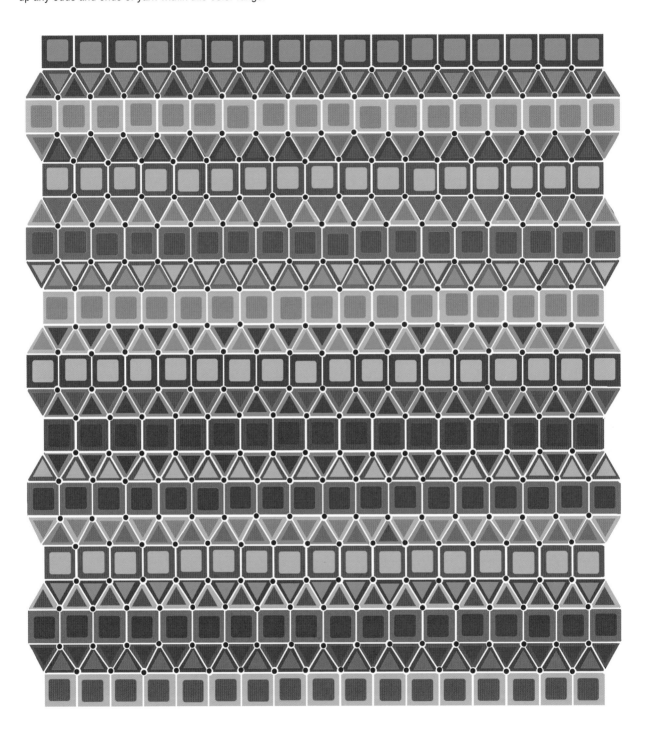

Color variations

For a warmer, richer palette, choose zingy pinks, cool purples and rich oranges, all tied together with calming yellow.

Rose Window

My rose window afghan is inspired by the stained-glass windows of the same name found in Gothic cathedrals. It's also a tribute and thank you to all my dyeing and spinning friends from the wool world. It contains yarn from Fyberspates, Easyknits, Skein Queen, The Knitting Goddess, John Arbon Textiles and some of The Natural Dye Studio. The base color is a raspberry pink, which was one of The Natural Dye Studio's core colors, dyed with cochineal. The afghan is started in the center and worked outwards.

Afghan size
Approximately 53 x 53in (135 x 135cm) across the middle

Hook size
3 or 3.25mm (US C/2 or D/3)

Yarn type
Fingering (4-ply) yarn: 390yd (360m) per 100g

Yarn notes
I made this afghan with oddments of yarn left over from other projects. If you prefer to buy new yarn, consider choosing the yarn brands below. You do not need to use the same dye lots.

Worldwide brands:
Drops: Alpaca, Alpaca/Silk
Fyberspates: Vivacious 4-ply
Cascade: 220 Fingering, Heritage Silk
Knit Picks: Palette yarn

UK independent dyers and spinners:
Skein Queen: Selkino, Lustrous
John Arbon Textiles: Exmoor Sock, Knit by Numbers 4-ply
Easyknits: Splendour
The Little Grey Sheep: Stein 4-ply

Color palette

Use up oddments and leftovers from other projects.

Gold: 150g

Orange: 200g

Soft red: 10g

Rose: 350g

Violet: 150g

Indigo: 100g

Jade: 150g

Green: 50g

Construction

JOINING: The finished squares are slip stitched or crocheted together along each side. Crochet into the corresponding gaps between the stitches on each side of the motif.

FINISHING: To create a border, work two rows of single crochet.

Color chart

This chart is designed to give you an overall look at how this afghan is composed, and how the colors interact with each other; there is further detail on the afghan's motif arrangement in the step-by-step section (pages 68–69). The most prominent color here is pink but you don't need to use the same colors as I have done. There are two other color variation charts for inspiration on pages 70 and 71.

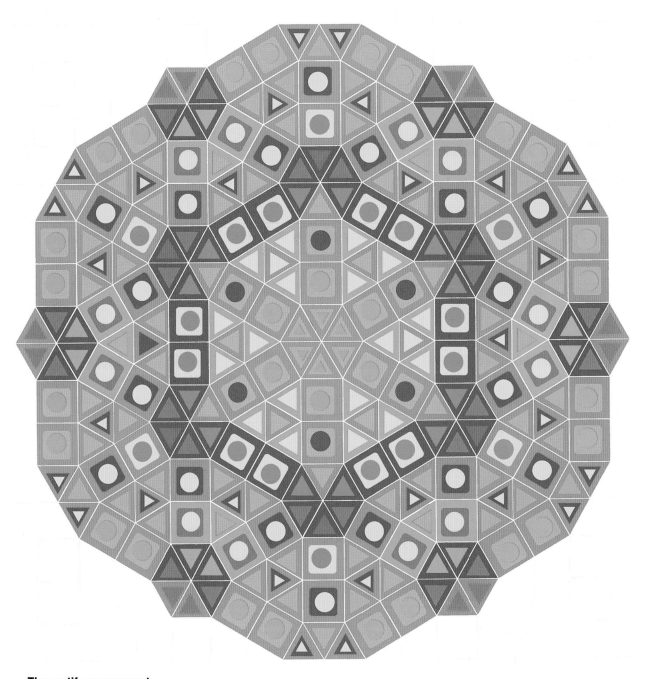

The motif arrangement

Square motif
3 x 3in (7.5 x 7.5cm)

Using color 1, make a 4-ch foundation chain and join in a ring with a sl st.

Round 1: 2 ch (counts as 1 hdc), 11 hdc in the foundation ring. Join to the 2nd st of original 2-ch with a sl st (12 hdc).

Round 2: in this and all following rounds work into the gaps between sts from the previous round. 2 ch (counts as 1 hdc), 1 hdc in same gap, *2 hdc in next gap*. Repeat from * to * 10 times. Join to the 2nd st of original 2-ch with a sl st (24 hdc). Fasten off.

Round 3: join color 2 where round 2 completed, 3 ch (counts as 1 dc) in the first gap, *1 hdc in next gap, 1 sc in the next 3 gaps, 1 hdc in next gap, (1 dc, 2 ch**, 1 dc) in next gap (this is a corner)*. Repeat from * to * 3 times, ending last repeat at **. Join to the 3rd st of original 3-ch with a sl st. Fasten off.

Round 4: join color 3 in any corner space, 2 ch (counts as 1 hdc), 1 hdc in the same corner space, *1 hdc in the next 6 gaps, (2 hdc, 2 ch**, 2 hdc) in corner space*. Repeat from * to * 3 times, ending last repeat at **. Join to the 2nd st of original 2-ch with a sl st.

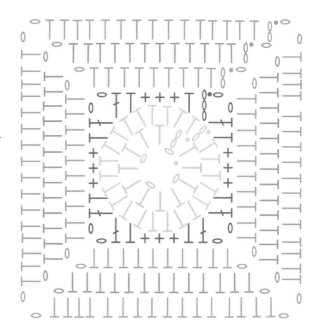

The motif stitch diagram

Round 5: 2 ch (counts as 1 hdc), 1 hdc in same gap (this is easier to do if you position the hook at a slight angle), 1 hdc in the next 9 gaps, (2 hdc, 2 ch**, 2 hdc) in corner space*. Repeat from * to * 3 times, ending last repeat at **. Join to the 2nd st of original 2-ch with a sl st. Fasten off.

Round 6: 2 ch (counts as 1 hdc), 1 hdc in same gap (this is easier to do if you position the hook at a slight angle), 1 hdc in the next 12 gaps, (2 hdc, 2 ch**, 2 hdc) in corner space*. Repeat from * to * 3 times, ending last repeat at **. Join to the 2nd st of original 2-ch with a sl st. Fasten off.

Triangle motif
3in (7.5cm) along each edge

Using color 1, make a 4-ch foundation chain and join in a ring with a sl st.

Round 1: 2 ch (counts as 1 hdc), 3 hdc in foundation ring, 2 ch, *4 hdc in foundation ring, 2 ch*. Repeat from * to * once. Join to the 2nd st of original 2-ch with a sl st.

Round 2: in this and all following rounds work into the gaps between sts from the previous round. 2 ch (counts as 1 hdc), *1 sc in next 3 gaps, (1 hdc, 1 dc, 2 ch, 1 dc**, 1 hdc) in next gap* (this forms the corner). Repeat from * to * twice ending last repeat at **. Join to the 2nd st of original 2-ch with a sl st. Fasten off.

Round 3: join color 2 to a 2-ch corner space, 2 ch (counts as 1 hdc), 1 hdc in same 2-ch corner. *1 hdc in next 6 gaps, (2 hdc, 2 ch**, 2 hdc) in corner space*. Repeat from * to * twice more ending the last repeat at **. Join to the 2nd st of original 2-ch with a sl st. Fasten off.

Round 4: join color 3 to a 2-ch corner space, 2 ch (counts as 1 hdc), 1 hdc in same 2-ch corner space, *1 hdc in next 9 gaps, (2 hdc, 2 ch**, 2 hdc) in next gap (this forms the corner)*. Repeat from * to * twice more ending the last repeat at **. Join to the 2nd st of original 2-ch with a sl st.

Round 5: 2 ch (counts as 1 hdc), 1 hdc in same 2-ch corner space (this is easier to do if you position your hook at a slight angle), *1 hdc in next 12 gaps, (2 hdc, 2 ch**, 2 hdc) in next gap (this forms the corner)*. Repeat from * to * twice more ending the last repeat at **. Join to the 2nd st of original 2-ch with a sl st. Fasten off.

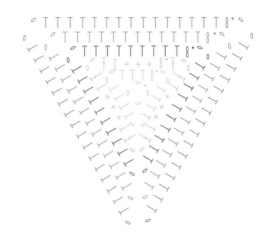

The motif stitch diagram

●●●●●●

The layout key

Motif	Rounds 1 & 2	Round 3	Round 4	Round 5	Round 6
Triangle motif 1: make 6	Jade	Orange	Rose	Rose	
Square motif 2: make 30	Jade	Gold	Orange	Orange	Rose
Triangle motif 3: make 18	Gold	Jade	Jade	Rose	
Triangle motif 4: make 66	Gold	Orange	Orange	Rose	Rose
Square motif 5: make 6	Violet	Gold	Orange	Orange	Rose
Triangle motif 6: make 12	Green	Violet	Violet	Indigo	
Square motif 7: make 12	Green	Gold	Violet	Violet	Indigo
Triangle motif 8: make 12	Indigo	Violet	Violet	Rose	
Triangle motif 9: make 6	Soft red	Violet	Violet	Indigo	
Square motif 10: make 6	Green	Gold	Rose	Rose	Rose
Square motif 11: make 18	Gold	Violet	Rose	Rose	Rose
Triangle motif 12: make 30	Gold	Violet	Rose	Rose	
Triangle motif 13: make 6	Orange	Jade	Jade	Rose	
Square motif 14: make 12	Gold	Indigo	Jade	Jade	Rose
Triangle motif 15: make 24	Jade	Violet	Violet	Indigo	
Triangle motif 16: make 12	Indigo	Violet	Rose	Rose	

Making Rose Window

1 Construction starts at the center of the afghan. Start with the six triangle Motif 1 blocks – slip stitch these into a hexagon.

2 Work outwards, building one layer of motifs at a time. Take six square Motif 2 blocks and slip stitch them in place.

3 Take six triangle Motif 3 blocks, six triangle Motif 4 blocks and six square Motif 5 blocks and slip stitch them in place.

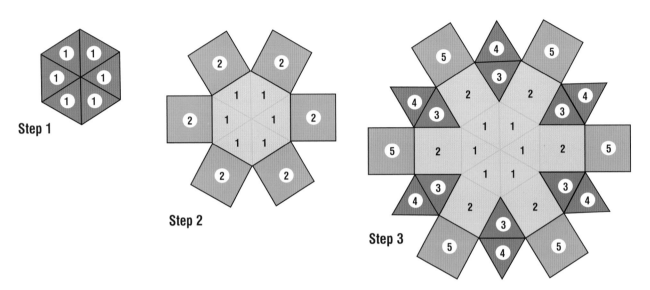

Step 1

Step 2

Step 3

4 Take twelve triangle Motif 3 blocks, six triangle Motif 4 blocks and twelve square Motif 7 blocks and slip stitch them in place.

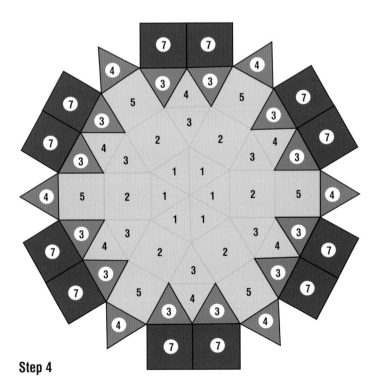

Step 4

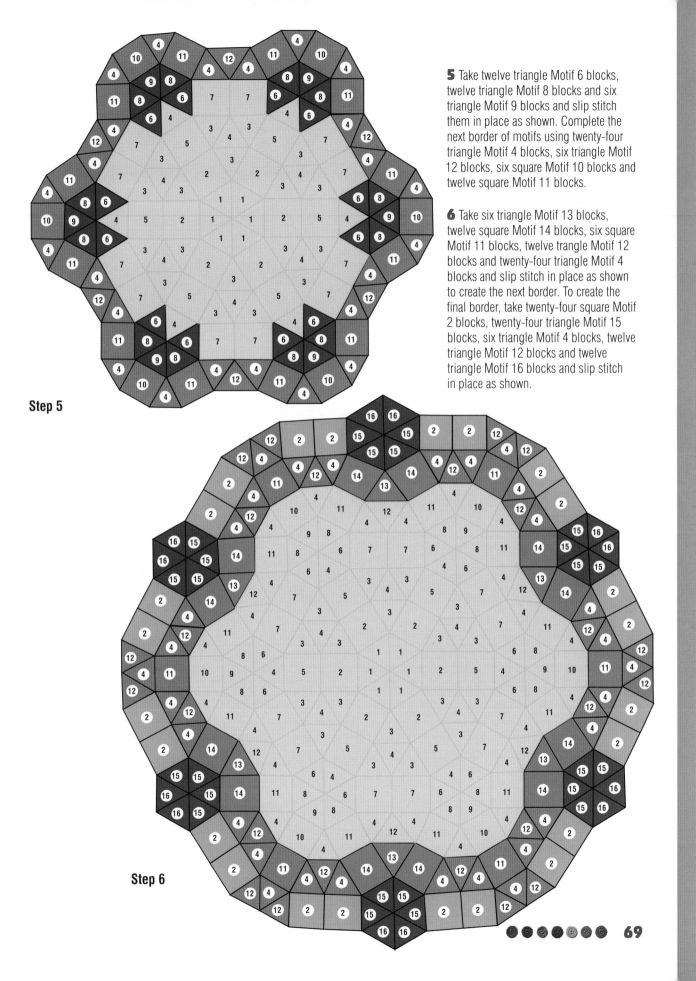

Step 5

Step 6

5 Take twelve triangle Motif 6 blocks, twelve triangle Motif 8 blocks and six triangle Motif 9 blocks and slip stitch them in place as shown. Complete the next border of motifs using twenty-four triangle Motif 4 blocks, six triangle Motif 12 blocks, six square Motif 10 blocks and twelve square Motif 11 blocks.

6 Take six triangle Motif 13 blocks, twelve square Motif 14 blocks, six square Motif 11 blocks, twelve trangle Motif 12 blocks and twenty-four triangle Motif 4 blocks and slip stitch in place as shown to create the next border. To create the final border, take twenty-four square Motif 2 blocks, twenty-four triangle Motif 15 blocks, six triangle Motif 4 blocks, twelve triangle Motif 12 blocks and twelve triangle Motif 16 blocks and slip stitch in place as shown.

Color variations

For this variation I removed the blue elements from the design and kept to within a narrow tonal range – the colorful accents of green and yellow provide touches of contrast.

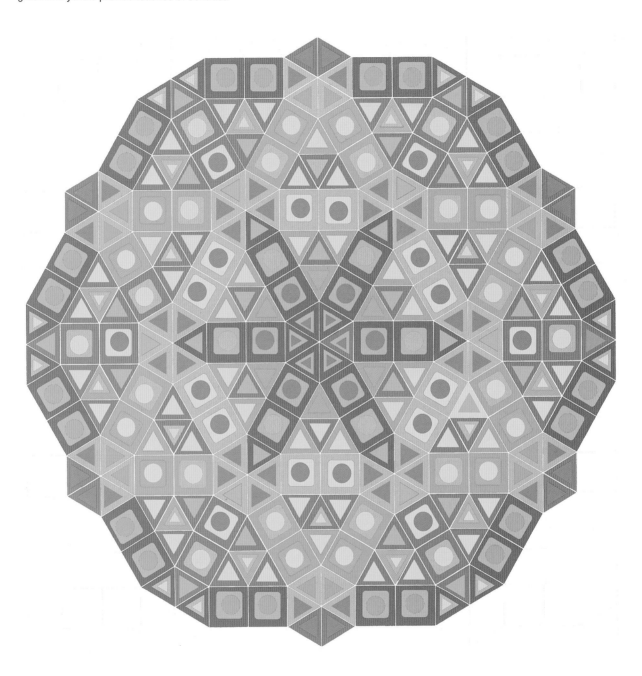

Color variations

I colored this design with jewel tones: vivid rubies, emeralds
and sapphires. Although there are lots of different colors used,
the balance of the design helps them to work well together.

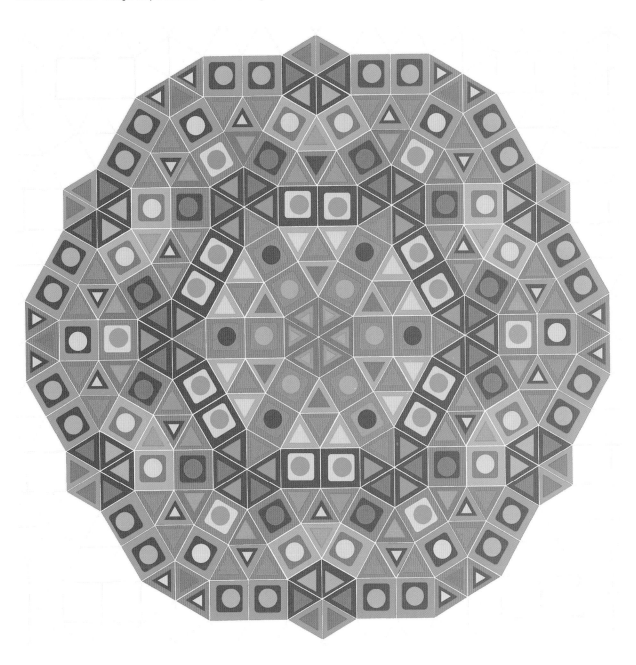

Knot Garden

This beautiful afghan was inspired by a patchwork quilt I made during the 1990s. It was originally inspired by Tudor knot gardens. A knot garden is laid out in a geometric pattern, and each flower bed is normally bordered with a box hedge. It was inspired by a visit to a quilt show at Hatfield House in Hertfordshire, UK. While at the quilt show, I took time out to visit the knot garden – the geometry and color made it perfect for a geometric design.

Afghan size
66 x 66in (168 x 168cm)

Hook size
3 or 3.25mm (UK C/2 or D/3)

Yarn type
Fingering (4-ply) yarn:
390yd (360m) per 100g

Yarn notes
I made this afghan with oddments of yarn left over from other projects. If you prefer to buy new yarn, consider choosing the yarn brands below. You do not need to use the same dye lots.

Color palette

Use scraps leftover from other projects; I recommend you use a collection of different shades for each color and alternate between them throughout the afghan for a more detailed feel.

Gold: 50g

Rose: 50g

Lilac: 450g

Currant: 350g

Heather: 450g

Azure: 550g

Worldwide brands:
Drops: Alpaca, Alpaca/Silk
Fyberspates: Vivacious 4-ply
Cascade: 220 Fingering, Heritage Silk
Knit Picks: Palette yarn

UK independent dyers and spinners:
Skein Queen: Selkino, Lustrous
John Arbon Textiles: Exmoor Sock, Knit by Numbers 4-ply
Easyknits: Splendour
The Little Grey Sheep: Stein 4-ply

Construction

JOINING: The finished squares are slip stitched or crocheted together along each side. Crochet into the corresponding gaps between the stitches on each side of the motif.

FINISHING: To create a border, work two rows of single crochet.

Color chart

This chart is designed to give you an overall look at how this afghan is composed, and how the colors interact with each other; there is further detail on the afghan's motif arrangement in the step-by-step section (pages 79–81). The most prominent color here is purple but you don't need to use the same colors as I have done. There are two other color variation charts for inspiration on pages 82 and 83.

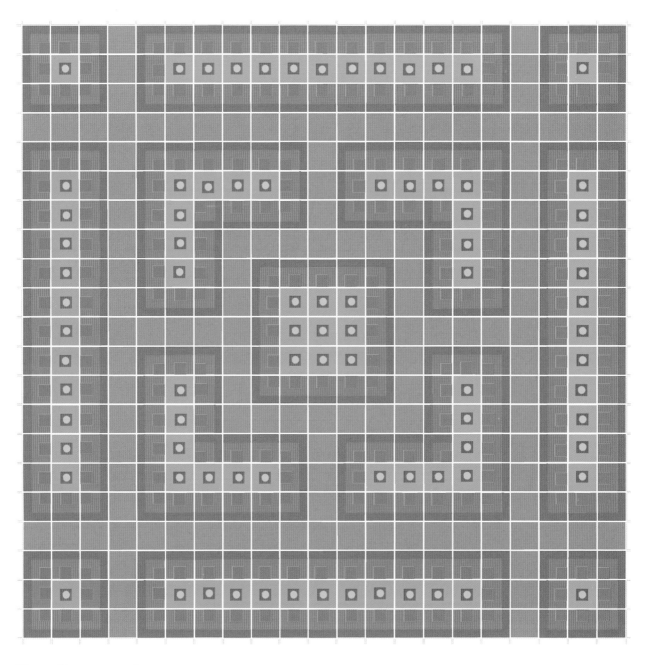

The motif arrangement

Square motif
3 x 3in (7.5 x 7.5cm)

Using color 1, make a 4-ch foundation chain and join in a ring with a sl st.

Round 1: 2 ch (counts as 1 hdc), 11 hdc in the foundation ring. Join to the 2nd st of original 2-ch with a sl st (12 hdc).

Round 2: in this and all following rounds work into the gaps between sts from the previous round. 2 ch (counts as 1 hdc), 1 hdc in same gap, *2 hdc in next gap*. Repeat from * to * 10 times. Join to the 2nd st of original 2-ch with a sl st (24 hdc). Fasten off.

Round 3: join color 2 where round 2 completed, 3 ch (counts as 1 dc) in the first gap, *1 hdc in next gap, 1 sc in the next 3 gaps, 1 hdc in next gap, (1 dc, 2 ch**, 1 dc) in next gap (this is a corner)*. Repeat from * to * 3 times, ending last repeat at **. Join to the 3rd st of original 3-ch with a sl st. Fasten off.

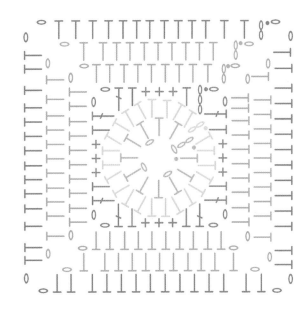

The motif stitch diagram

Round 4: join color 3 in any corner space, 2 ch (counts as 1 hdc), 1 hdc in the same corner space, *1 hdc in the next 6 gaps, (2 hdc, 2 ch**, 2 hdc) in corner space*. Repeat from * to * 3 times, ending last repeat at **. Join to the 2nd st of original 2-ch with a sl st.

Round 5: 2 ch (counts as 1 hdc), 1 hdc in same gap (this is easier to do if you position the hook at a slight angle), 1 hdc in the next 9 gaps, (2 hdc, 2 ch**, 2 hdc) in corner space*. Repeat from * to * 3 times, ending last repeat at **. Join to the 2nd st of original 2-ch with a sl st.

Round 6: 2 ch (counts as 1 hdc), 1 hdc in same gap (this is easier to do if you position the hook at a slight angle), 1 hdc in the next 12 gaps, (2 hdc, 2 ch**, 2 hdc) in corner space*. Repeat from * to * 3 times, ending last repeat at **. Join to the 2nd st of original 2-ch with a sl st. Fasten off.

Three-quarter square motif

3 x 3in (7.5 x 7.5cm)

Using color 1, make a 4-ch foundation chain and join in a ring with a sl st.

Round 1: 2 ch (counts as 1 hdc), 11 hdc in the foundation ring. Join to the 2nd st of original 2-ch with a sl st (12 hdc).

Round 2: in this and all following rounds work into the gaps between sts from the previous round. 2 ch (counts as 1 hdc), 1 hdc in same gap, *2 hdc in next gap*. Repeat from * to * 10 times. Join to the 2nd st of original 2-ch with a sl st (24 hdc).

Round 3: (3 ch (counts as 1 dc), 2 ch, 1 dc) in the first gap (this is a corner), *1 hdc in next gap, 1 sc in the next 3 gaps, 1 hdc in next gap**, (1 dc, 2 ch, 1 dc) in next gap (this is a corner)*. Repeat from * to * 3 times, ending last repeat at **. Join to the 3rd st of original 3-ch with a sl st. Fasten off.

Round 4: join color 2 in any corner space, 2 ch (counts as 1 hdc), 1 hdc in the same corner space, *1 hdc in the next 6 gaps, (2 hdc**, 2 ch, 2 hdc) in corner space*. Repeat from * to * twice, ending last repeat at **. Turn.

Round 5: Join color 3 in last hdc from round 4, 2 ch (counts as 1 hdc), miss one gap, 1 hdc in the next 8 gaps, (2 hdc, 2 ch, 2 hdc) in corner space. 1 hdc in the next 9 gaps, (2 hdc, 2 ch, 2 hdc) in corner space. 1 hdc in the next 8 gaps, miss one gap, 1 hdc in top of 2-ch. Turn.

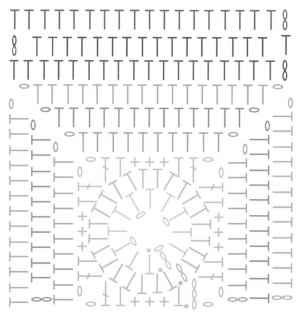

The motif stitch diagram

Round 6: 2 ch (counts as 1 hdc), 1 hdc in the next 10 gaps, (2 hdc, 2 ch, 2 hdc) in corner space. 1 hdc in the next 12 gaps, (2 hdc, 2 ch, 2 hdc) in corner space. 1 hdc in the next 10 gaps, 1 hdc in top of 2-ch. Fasten off.

Row 7: Join color 4 in top right corner space of round 6, 2 ch (counts as 1 hdc), 1 hdc in same gap, 1 hdc in the next 15 gaps, 2 hdc in corner space. Turn.

Row 8: 2 ch (counts as 1 hdc), miss one gap, 1 hdc in the next 16 gaps, 1 hdc in top of 2-ch. Turn.

Row 9: 2 ch (counts as 1 hdc), 1 hdc in the next 17 gaps, 1 hdc in top of 2-ch. Fasten off.

Miter square motif

3 x 3in (7.5 x 7.5cm)

Using color 1, make a 4-ch foundation chain and join in a ring with a sl st.

Round 1: 2 ch (counts as 1 hdc), 11 hdc in the foundation ring. Join to the 2nd st of original 2-ch with a sl st (12 hdc).

Round 2: in this and all following rounds work into the gaps between sts from the previous round. 2 ch (counts as 1 hdc), 1 hdc in same gap, *2 hdc in next gap*. Repeat from * to * 10 times. Join to the 2nd st of original 2-ch with a sl st (24 hdc).

Round 3: (3 ch (counts as 1 dc), 2 ch, 1 dc) in the first gap (this is a corner), *1 hdc in next gap, 1 sc in the next 3 gaps, 1 hdc in next gap**, (1 dc, 2 ch, 1 dc) in next gap (this is a corner)*. Repeat from * to * 3 times, ending last repeat at **. Join to the 3rd st of original 3-ch with a sl st. Fasten off.

Round 4: join color 2 in any corner space, 2 ch (counts as 1 hdc), 1 hdc in the same corner space, 1 hdc in the next 6 gaps, (2 hdc, 2 ch, 2 hdc) in corner space, 1 hdc in next 6 gaps, 2 hdc in corner space. Fasten off. Turn.

Round 5: join color 3 in last hdc from round 4, 2 ch (counts as 1 hdc), miss one gap, 1 hdc in the next 8 gaps, (2 hdc, 2 ch, 2 hdc) in corner space, 1 hdc in the next 9 gaps. Turn.

Row 6: 2 ch (counts as 1 hdc), 1 hdc in the next 10 gaps, (2 hdc, 2 ch, 2 hdc) in corner space, 1 hdc in next 10 gaps, 1 hdc in top of 2-ch. Fasten off. Turn.

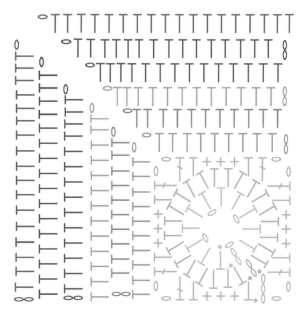

The motif stitch diagram

Row 7: join color 4 in last hdc from round 6, 2 ch (counts as 1 hdc), 1 hdc in the next 12 gaps, (2 hdc, 2 ch, 2 hdc) in corner space, 1 hdc in the next 12 gaps, 1 hdc in top of 2-ch. Turn.

Row 8: 2 ch (counts as 1 hdc), miss one gap, 1 hdc in the next 13 gaps, (2 hdc, 2 ch, 2 hdc) in corner space, 1 hdc in next 14 gaps. Turn.

Row 9: 2 ch (counts as 1 hdc), 1 hdc in the next 15 gaps, (2 hdc, 2 ch, 2 hdc) in corner space, 1 hdc in the next 15 gaps, 1 hdc in top of 2-ch. Fasten off.

The layout key

Motif	Round 1	Round 2	Round 3	Round 4	Round 5	Round 6	Rounds 7, 8 & 9
Square motif 1: make 85	Gold	Rose	Lilac	Azure	Azure	Gold	
Three-quarter square motif 2: make 180	Azure	Azure	Azure	Currant	Currant	Currant	Heather
Miter square motif 3: make 60	Azure	Azure	Azure	Currant	Currant	Currant	Heather
Square motif 4: make 116	Lilac	Lilac	Lilac	Lilac	Lilac	Azure	

Making Knot Garden

1 Knot Garden is started at the center and then rounds of motifs are built up around this. Create nine Motif 1 blocks and slip stitch them together as shown.

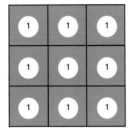

Step 1

2 Take twelve Motif 2 blocks and four Motif 3 blocks and slip stitch them in place to form the first border. On the diagram below, the purple line indicates how the dark purple band on each of the motifs should align.

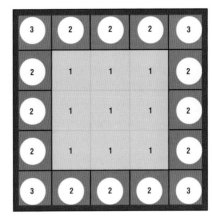

Step 2

3 Take twenty-four Motif 4 blocks and slip stitch them in place to create the second border. To create the third border, take four Motif 4 blocks, twelve Motif 3 blocks and sixteen Motif 2 blocks; slip stitch them in place as shown.

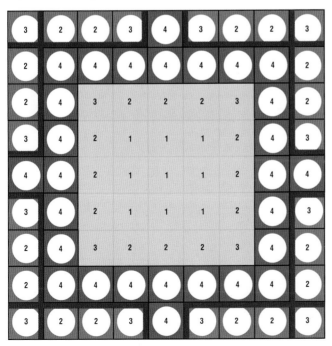

Step 3

4 Take four Motif 4 blocks, eight Motif 2 blocks and twenty-eight Motif 1 blocks, and slip stitch in place as shown to create the fourth border.

5 For the fifth border you will need: four Motif 4 blocks, twelve Motif 3 blocks and thirty-two Motif 2 blocks.

6 Use fifty-six Motif 4 blocks to complete the sixth border.

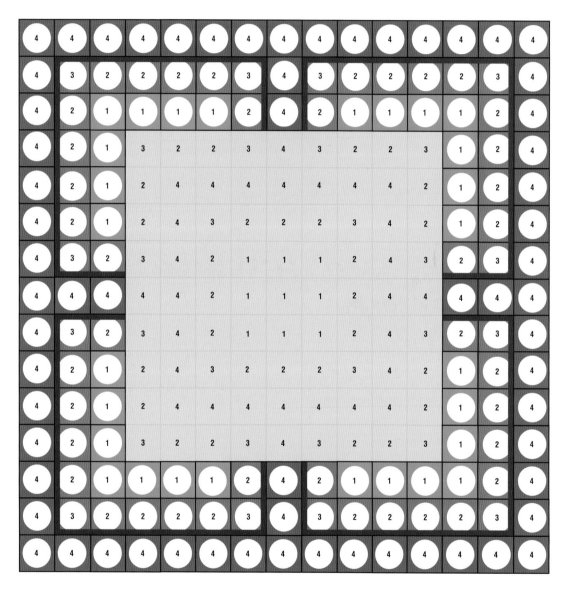

Steps 4–6

7 To create the seventh border, take twelve Motif 3 blocks, eight Motif 4 blocks and forty-four Motif 2 blocks. Slip stitch them in place as shown.

8 For the eighth border, slip stitch forty-eight Motif 1 blocks, sixteen Motif 2 blocks and eight Motif 4 blocks in place as shown.

9 For the final border, take eight Motif 4 blocks, twenty Motif 3 blocks and fifty-two Motif 2 blocks and slip stitch them in place as shown.

Steps 7–9

Color variations

Swap the pinks and purples for a range of vibrant tones: magenta, cyan, lime and orange. These vivid tones work well together and create an afghan that will bring plenty of warmth to an indoor space.

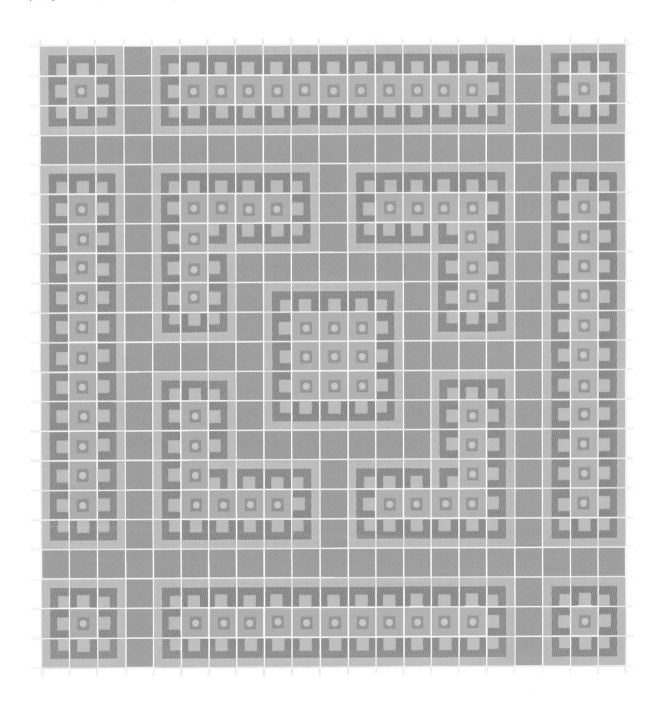

Color variations

Introduce more foliage to your garden: complement the bright green elements with a deep, calming purple that runs through the channels of the design.

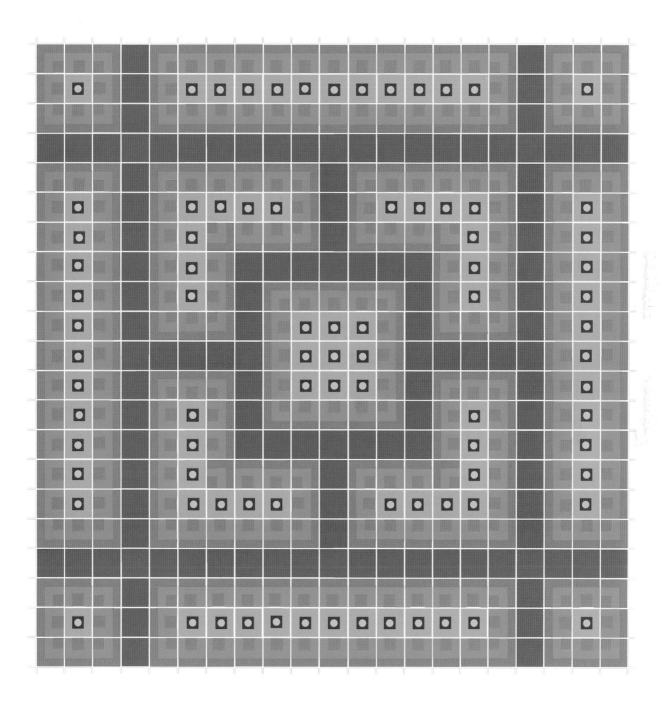

Flying Geese

I love the colors and shapes used in traditional quilts and this design was inspired by the traditional American quilt block of the same name. It is claimed Flying Geese quilts were hung on washing lines as part of the Underground Railroad Quilt Code; the Underground Railroad was a network of secret routes used by American slaves to escape from the southern states, where slavery was legal, to the free northern states and Canada. The points of the triangles (geese) pointed in the direction that the slaves should travel on their secret journey north. Even if this is just a myth, it's nice to imagine that a quilt could not only be comfort against the cold, but also a helpful tool against slavery.

Afghan size
47 x 57in (119.5 x 145cm)

Hook size
3 or 3.25mm (US C/2 or D/3)

Yarn type
Fingering (4-ply) yarn:
390yd (360m) per 100g

Yarn notes
I made this afghan with oddments of yarn left over from other projects. If you prefer to buy new yarn, consider choosing the yarn brands below. You do not need to use the same dye lots.

Color palette

Use scraps leftover from other projects; I recommend you use a collection of different shades for each color and alternate between them throughout the afghan for a more detailed feel.

Dark indigo: 600g

Jade, two shades: 50g

Green, two shades: 50g

Lime, two shades: 50g

Gold, two shades: 50g

Orange, three shades: 75g

Soft red, two shades: 50g

Rose, two shades: 50g

Violet, three shades: 75g

Worldwide brands:
Drops: Alpaca, Alpaca/Silk
Fyberspates: Vivacious 4-ply
Cascade: 220 Fingering, Heritage Silk
Knit Picks: Palette yarn
Madelinetosh: Tosh Merino Light

UK independent dyers and spinners:
Skein Queen: Selkino, Lustrous
John Arbon Textiles: Exmoor Sock, Knit by Numbers 4-ply
Easyknits: Splendour
The Little Grey Sheep: Stein 4-ply

Construction

JOINING: The finished triangles are slip stitched or crocheted together along each side. Crochet into the corresponding gaps between the stitches on each side of the motif.

FINISHING: To create a border, work two rows of single crochet.

Color chart

This chart is designed to give you an overall look at how this afghan is composed, and how the colors interact with each other; there is further detail on the afghan's motif arrangement in the step-by-step section (pages 90–91). The most prominent color here is blue but you don't need to use the same colors as I have done. There are two other variation charts for inspiration on pages 92 and 93.

The motif arrangement

Triangle motif

4in (10cm) along each side from point to point

Using color 1, make a 4-ch foundation chain and join in a ring with a sl st.

Round 1: 2 ch (counts as 1 hdc), 3 hdc in foundation ring, 2 ch, *4 hdc in foundation ring, 2 ch*. Repeat from * to * once. Join to the 2nd st of original 2-ch with a sl st.

Round 2: in this and all following rounds work into the gaps between sts from the previous round. 2 ch (counts as 1 hdc), *1 sc in next 3 gaps, (1 hdc, 1 dc, 2 ch, 1 dc**, 1 hdc) in next gap* (this forms the corner). Repeat from * to * twice ending last repeat at **. Join to the 2nd st of original 2-ch with a sl st. Fasten off.

Triangle points: crochet on each side of the triangle.
Row 1: Join color 2 to any 2-ch corner space, 2 ch, 1 sc in the same corner space, 1 sc in the next 6 gaps, 2 sc into next 2-ch corner. Turn.
Row 2: 1 ch, miss one gap, 1 sc into each gap to end.
Rows 3–9: Repeat Row 2.
Fasten off.

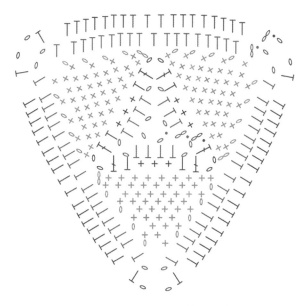

The motif stitch diagram

Round 3: join color 1 to a triangle point in the middle of the ch and the sc, 2 ch (counts as 1 hdc) in the same space, *1 hdc into next 8 row ends, 1 hdc into the 2-ch corner from the center triangle, 1 hdc into the next 8 row ends, (1 hdc, 2 ch**, 1 hdc) in the middle of the triangle corner between the ch and the sc*. Repeat from * to * twice, ending the last repeat at **. Join to the 2nd st of original 2-ch with a sl st (19 hdc on each side).

Round 4: 2 ch (counts as 1 hdc) in the first 2-ch corner, 1 hdc in next 18 gaps, (1 hdc, 2 ch**, 1 hdc) in the 2-ch corner space*. Repeat from * to * twice ending the last repeat at **. Join to the 2nd st of original 2-ch with a sl st (20 hdc on each side). Fasten off. Use the tail end to crochet or sew to the adjoining motif.

Two-pointed triangle edging motif

4in (10cm) along the bottom edge, 2in (5cm) along the top edge, 2½in (6.5cm) on the sides

Using color 1, make a 4-ch foundation chain and join in a ring with a sl st.

Round 1: 2 ch (counts as 1 hdc), 3 hdc in foundation ring, 2 ch, *4 hdc in foundation ring, 2 ch*. Repeat from * to * once. Join to the 2nd st of original 2-ch with a sl st.

Round 2: in this and all following rounds work into the gaps between sts from the previous round. 2 ch (counts as 1 hdc), *1 sc in next 3 gaps, (1 hdc, 1 dc, 2 ch, 1 dc**, 1 hdc) in next gap* (this forms the corner). Repeat from * to * twice ending last repeat at **. Join to the 2nd st of original 2-ch with a sl st.

Triangle points: crochet on two sides of the triangle.
Row 1: join color 2 to any 2-ch corner space, 2 ch, 1 sc in the same corner space, 1 sc in the next 6 gaps, 2 sc into next 2-ch corner. Turn.
Row 2: 1 ch, miss one gap, 1 sc into each gap to end.
Rows 3–9: Repeat Row 2.
Fasten off.

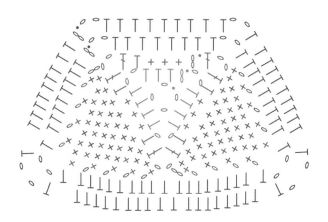

The motif stitch diagram

Round 3: join color 1 to the top left original triangle point, 2 ch (counts as 1 hdc), 1 hdc into next 8 row ends, (1 hdc, 2 ch, 1 hdc) in the middle of the triangle corner between the ch and the sc, 1 hdc into next 8 row ends, 1 hdc into the 2-ch corner from the center triangle, 1 hdc into next 8 row ends, (1 hdc, 2 ch, 1 hdc) in the middle of the triangle corner between the ch and the sc, 1 hdc into next 8 row ends, (1 hdc, 2 ch, 1 hdc) in top right original triangle point, 1 hdc in next 6 gaps, 1 hdc in corner space, 2ch. Join to the 2nd st of original 2-ch with a sl st (19 hdc on bottom edge).

Round 4: 2 ch (counts as 1 hdc), 1 hdc into next 9 gaps, (1 hdc, 2 ch, 1 hdc) in the 2-ch corner space, 1 hdc into next 18 gaps, (1 hdc, 2 ch, 1 hdc) in the 2-ch corner space, 1 hdc into next 9 gaps, (1 hdc, 2 ch, 1 hdc) in the 2-ch corner space, 1 hdc into next 7 gaps, 1 hdc in corner space, 2ch. Join to the 2nd st of original 2-ch with a sl st (20 hdc on bottom edge).

The layout key

Motif	Rounds 1 & 2	Triangle points	Rounds 3 & 4
Background triangle motif: make 104	Dark indigo	Dark indigo	Dark indigo
Triangle motif 1: make 7	Dark indigo	Jade (shade 1)	Dark indigo
Triangle motif 2: make 6	Dark indigo	Jade (shade 2)	Dark indigo
Triangle motif 3: make 7	Dark indigo	Green (shade 1)	Dark indigo
Triangle motif 4: make 6	Dark indigo	Green (shade 2)	Dark indigo
Triangle motif 5: make 7	Dark indigo	Lime (shade 1)	Dark indigo
Triangle motif 6: make 6	Dark indigo	Lime (shade 2)	Dark indigo
Triangle motif 7: make 7	Dark indigo	Gold (shade 1)	Dark indigo
Triangle motif 8: make 7	Dark indigo	Gold (shade 2)	Dark indigo
Triangle motif 9: make 7	Dark indigo	Orange (shade 1)	Dark indigo
Triangle motif 10: make 6	Dark indigo	Orange (shade 2)	Dark indigo

Motif	Rounds 1 & 2	Triangle points	Rounds 3 & 4
Triangle motif 11: make 7	Dark indigo	Orange (shade 3)	Dark indigo
Triangle motif 12: make 6	Dark indigo	Soft red (shade 1)	Dark indigo
Triangle motif 13: make 6	Dark indigo	Soft red (shade 2)	Dark indigo
Triangle motif 14: make 6	Dark indigo	Rose (shade 1)	Dark indigo
Triangle motif 15: make 7	Dark indigo	Rose (shade 2)	Dark indigo
Triangle motif 16: make 6	Dark indigo	Violet (shade 1)	Dark indigo
Triangle motif 17: make 7	Dark indigo	Violet (shade 2)	Dark indigo
Triangle motif 18: make 6	Dark indigo	Violet (shade 3)	Dark indigo
Background 2-pointed triangle motif: make 26	Dark indigo	Dark indigo	Dark indigo

Making Flying Geese

1 This afghan is constructed in strips: start from the top of the afghan and then add a strip at a time. Take eight triangles, two 2-pointed triangles and one block each of Motif 1, Motif 11, Motif 3, Motif 14, Motif 5, Motif 15, Motif 7, Motif 17 and Motif 9 – slip stitch together as shown.

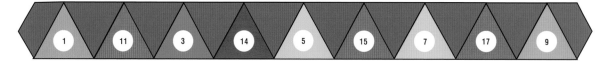

Step 1

2 For the second row, take eight triangles, two 2-pointed triangles and one block each of Motif 2, Motif 12, Motif 4, Motif 15, Motif 6, Motif 16, Motif 8, Motif 18 and Motif 10; slip stitch together as shown.

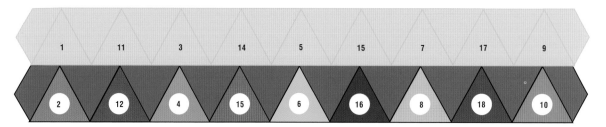

Step 2

3 Complete the rest of the afghan in the same way, working one row at a time. In total you will need six Motif 1 blocks, five Motif 2 blocks, six Motif 3 blocks, five Motif 4 blocks, six Motif 5 blocks, five Motif 6 blocks, six Motif 7 blocks, six Motif 8 blocks, six Motif 9 blocks, five Motif 10 blocks, six Motif 11 blocks, five Motif 12 blocks, six motif 13 blocks, five Motif 14 blocks, five Motif 15 blocks, five Motif 16 blocks, six Motif 17 blocks and five Motif 18 blocks.

Step 3

Color variations

For this variation I arranged the motifs so that the rainbow pattern spreads diagonally across the afghan.

Color variations

For this variation I created two basic column designs, with the rainbows progressing from blue to purple and orange to yellow, then alternated them across the whole design.

Mirage

Mirage is a re-make of a quilt I made in the 1990s, called Reflection of a Mirage, which was originally inspired by historical Turkish city maps. The center panel of the afghan depicts the reflection of a desert city. I can't remember why there was a reflection, but as I love the way the shapes fit together I decided to stick to the original name and design. The base color is turquoise and fits into the rainbow in place of blue. For me, turquoise is the color of the Mediterranean and works nicely with orange, which is the color used in Persian carpets, which also form part of the inspiration.

Afghan size
53 x 53in (135 x 135cm)

Hook size
4mm (US G/6)

Yarn type
DK (8-ply) yarn: 263–273yd (240–250m) per 100g

Yarn notes
I made this afghan with oddments of yarn left over from other projects. If you prefer to buy new yarn, consider choosing the yarn brands below. You do not need to use the same dye lots.

Worldwide brands:
Fyberspates: Vivacious DK
Cascade: 220 Sport
Knit Picks: Wool of the Andes Sport
Yarn Stories: Merino DK, Merino/Alpaca DK

UK independent dyers and spinners:
John Arbon Textiles: Knit by Numbers DK

Color palette

Use oddments and leftovers from other projects.

Gold: 100g

Orange: 100g

Scarlet: 200g

Rose, two shades: 100g

Violet: 100g

Lavender: 200g

Azure, three shades: 600g

Apple, three shades: 100g

Construction

Mirage is started with the central column and then worked on both sides and outwards to the edges.

JOINING: The finished squares are slip stitched or crocheted together along each side. Crochet into the corresponding gaps between the stitches on each side of the motif.

FINISHING: To create a border, work two rows of half double crochet.

Color chart

This chart is designed to give you an overall look at how this afghan is composed, and how the colors interact with each other; there is further detail on the afghan's motif arrangement in the step-by-step section (pages 102–103). The most prominent color here is turquoise but you don't need to use the same colors as I have done. There are two other color variation charts for inspiration on pages 104 and 105.

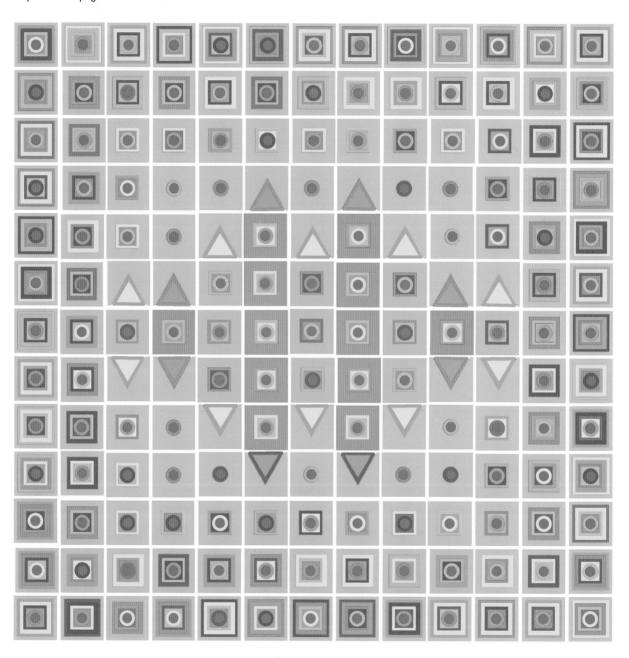

The motif arrangement

Square motif
4 x 4in (10 x 10cm)

Using color 1, make a 4-ch foundation chain and join in a ring with a sl st.

Round 1: 2 ch (counts as 1 hdc), 11 hdc in the foundation ring. Join to the 2nd st of original 2-ch with a sl st (12 hdc). Fasten off.

Round 2: in this and all following rounds work into the gaps between sts from the previous round. Join color 2 where round 1 completed, 2 ch (counts as 1 hdc),1 hdc in same gap, *2 hdc in next gap*. Repeat from * to * 10 times. Join to the 2nd st of original 2-ch with a sl st (24 hdc). Fasten off.

Round 3: join color 3 where round 2 completed, 3 ch (counts as 1 dc) in the first gap, *1 hdc in next gap, 1 sc in the next 3 gaps, 1 hdc in next gap, (1 dc, 2 ch**, 1 dc) in next gap (this is a corner)*. Repeat from * to * 3 times, ending last repeat at **. Join to the 3rd st of original 3-ch with a sl st. Fasten off.

Round 4: join color 4 in any corner space, 2 ch (counts as 1 hdc), 1 hdc in the same corner space, *1 hdc in the next 6 gaps, (2 hdc, 2 ch**, 2 hdc) in corner space*. Repeat from * to * 3 times, ending last repeat at **. Join to the 2nd st of original 2-ch with a sl st. Fasten off.

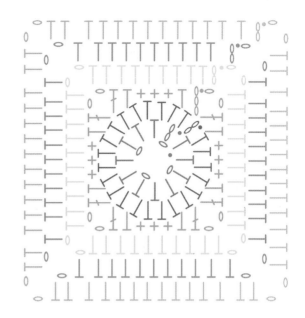

The motif stitch diagram

Round 5: join color 5 in any corner space, 2 ch (counts as 1 hdc), 1 hdc in the next 9 gaps, (1 hdc, 2 ch**, 1 hdc) in corner space*. Repeat from * to * 3 times, ending last repeat at **. Join to the 2nd st of original 2-ch with a sl st. Fasten off.

Round 6: join color 6 in any corner space, 2 ch (counts as 1 hdc), 1 hdc in same gap, 1 hdc in the next 10 gaps, (2 hdc, 2 ch**, 2 hdc) in corner space*. Repeat from * to * 3 times, ending last repeat at **. Join to the 2nd st of original 2-ch with a sl st. Fasten off.

Triangle in square motif

4 x 4in (10 x 10cm)

Using color 1, make a 4-ch foundation chain and join in a ring with a sl st.

Round 1: 2 ch (counts as 1 hdc), 3 hdc in foundation ring, 2 ch, *4 hdc in foundation ring, 2 ch*. Repeat from * to * once. Join to the 2nd st of original 2-ch with a sl st. Fasten off.

Round 2: in this and all following rounds work into the gaps between sts from the previous round. Join color 2 in any 2-ch space, 2 ch (counts as 1 hdc), *1 sc in next 3 gaps, (1 hdc, 1 dc, 2 ch, 1 dc**, 1 hdc) in next gap* (this forms the corner). Repeat from * to * twice ending last repeat at **. Join to the 2nd st of original 2-ch with a sl st. Fasten off.

Round 3: join color 3 to a 2-ch corner space, 2 ch (counts as 1 hdc), 1 sc in same 2-ch corner. *1 sc in next 6 gaps, (1 sc, 1 hdc, 2 ch**, 1 hdc, 1 sc) in corner space*. Repeat from * to * twice more ending the last repeat at **. Join to the 2nd st of original 2-ch with a sl st. Fasten off.

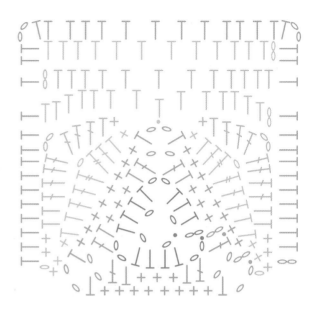

The motif stitch diagram

Triangle in square

Round 4 (background): join color 4 to a 2-ch corner space, 1 ch (counts as 1 sc), 1 sc in same gap, 1 sc in next gap, 1 hdc in next 2 gaps, 1 dc in next 2 gaps, (1 tr, 2 ch, 1 tr) in next gap, which will become a corner of the square, 1 dc in next gap, 1 hdc in next gap, 1 sc in next gap, 1 sl st in 2-ch corner of the triangle, 1 sc in next gap, 1 hdc in next gap, 1 dc in next gap, (1 tr, 2 ch, 1 tr) in next gap, which will become a corner of the square, 1 dc in next 2 gaps, 1 hdc in next 2 gaps, 1 sc in next gap, 2 sc in the 2-ch corner of the triangle. Turn.

Round 5: 1 ch (counts as 1 sc), miss one gap, 1 sc into the next 2 gaps, 1 hdc in next 2 gaps, 1 dc in next 2 gaps, (2 dc, 2 ch, 2 dc) in 2-ch corner space, 1 dc in next gap, 1 hdc in next gap, 1 sc in next gap, miss 1 gap, 1 hdc in 2-ch corner of triangle, (over the top of the sl st from round 4), miss 1 gap, 1 sc in next gap, 1 hdc in next gap, 1 dc in next gap, (2 dc, 2 ch, 2 dc) in 2-ch corner space, 1 dc in next 2 gaps, 1 hdc in next 2 gaps, 1 sc in next 3 gaps. Fasten off.

Row 6: work across the top of the square. Rejoin color 4 to top right corner space, 2 ch (counts as 1 hdc), 1 hdc in same gap, 1 hdc in next 10 gaps, 2 hdc in next 2-ch corner. Turn.

Row 7: 2 ch (counts as 1 hdc), miss 1 gap, 1 hdc in next 12 gaps. Turn.

Row 8: 2 ch (counts as 1 hdc), 1 hdc in next 12 gaps. Fasten off.

Round 9: Rejoin color 4 between 2 sc in bottom right corner of round 5, 2 ch (counts as 1 hdc), 1 hdc in next 7 gaps, 2 hdc into 2-ch corner from round 5, 1 hdc in the next 2 row ends, (2 hdc, 2 ch, 2 hdc) in last row end, 1 hdc in next 10 gaps, (2 hdc, 2 ch, 2 hdc) in row end, 1 hdc in next 2 row ends, 2 hdc in 2-ch corner from round 5, 1 hdc in next 8 gaps. Fasten off.

The layout key

The colors of the afghan are all chosen from color families rather than exact colors. Scarlet is used for round 1 in every case; the rest of the round colors are chosen from the color families shown below. The afghan works best if you have several similar shades of the same color, which makes it an ideal scrap afghan.

Motif	Round 1	Round 2	Round 3	Round 4	Round 5	Round 6	Rounds 7, 8 & 9
Square motif 1: make 11	Scarlet	Pink, red or orange	Pink, red or orange	Apple (shade 1)	Apple (shade 2)	Apple (shade 3)	
Square motif 2: make 12	Scarlet	Apple (shade 2)	Apple (shade 3)	Pink, red, or orange	Pink, red, or orange	Pink, red, or orange	
Triangle in square motif 3: make 10	Scarlet	Apple (shade 3)	Apple (shade 1)	Blue (shade 1)	Blue (shade 3)	Blue (shade 2)	Blue (shade 1)
Triangle in square motif 4: make 8	Scarlet	Apple (shade 2)	Pink, red, or orange	Blue (shade 2)	Blue (shade 1)	Blue (shade 3)	Blue (shade 2)
Square motif 5: make 14	Scarlet	Yellow, orange, red, green or pink	Blue (shade 3)	Blue (shade 1)	Blue (shade 2)	Blue (shade 1)	
Square motif 6: make 26	Scarlet	Yellow, orange, red, green or pink	Yellow, orange, red, green or pink	Blue (shade 3)	Blue (shade 1)	Blue (shade 3)	
Square motif 7: make 40	Scarlet	Yellow, orange, red, green or pink	Yellow, orange, red, green or pink	Yellow, orange, red, green or pink	Blue (shade 3)	Blue (shade 2)	
Square motif 8: make 48	Scarlet	Yellow, orange, red, green or pink	Yellow, orange, red, green or pink	Yellow, orange, red, green or pink	Yellow, orange, red, green or pink	Blue (shade 1)	

Making Mirage

1 Slip stitch together three Motif 1 blocks, two Motif 3 blocks and two Motif five blocks to form a column. Position the Motif 3 blocks as shown, with the triangles pointing correctly.

2 Add a further column on either side: slip stitch four Motif 4 blocks and ten Motif 2 blocks as shown.

3 Continue to work outwards a column at a time. Add eight Motif 1 blocks, two Motif 2 blocks, eight Motif 3 blocks, four Motif 4 blocks, twelve Motif 5 blocks and eight Motif 6 blocks.

Step 1

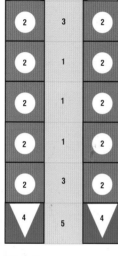

Step 2

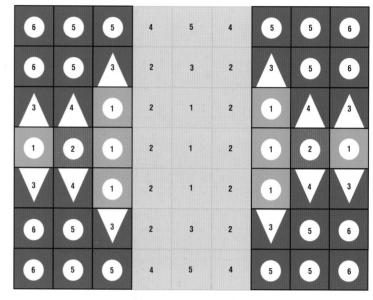

Step 3

4 With your central panel complete, slip stitch a row of Motif 6 blocks along the top and bottom edges: you will need eighteen in total.

Step 4

6	6	6	6	6	6	6	6	6
6	5	5	4	5	4	5	5	6
6	5	3	2	3	2	3	5	6
3	4	1	2	1	2	1	4	3
1	2	1	2	1	2	1	2	1
3	4	1	2	1	2	1	4	3
6	5	3	2	3	2	3	5	6
6	5	5	4	5	4	5	5	6
6	6	6	6	6	6	6	6	6

5 To complete the afghan you will create two borders of motifs around your central panel. The first border is made up of forty Motif 7 blocks; the second is made up of forty-eight Motif 8 blocks. Slip stitch them in place one border at a time.

8	8	8	8	8	8	8	8	8	8	8	8	8
8	7	7	7	7	7	7	7	7	7	7	7	8
8	7	6	6	6	6	6	6	6	6	6	7	8
8	7	6	5	5	4	5	4	5	5	6	7	8
8	7	6	5	3	2	3	2	3	5	6	7	8
8	7	3	4	1	2	1	2	1	4	3	7	8
8	7	1	2	1	2	1	2	1	2	1	7	8
8	7	3	4	1	2	1	2	1	4	3	7	8
8	7	6	5	3	2	3	2	3	5	6	7	8
8	7	6	5	5	4	5	4	5	5	6	7	8
8	7	6	6	6	6	6	6	6	6	6	7	8
8	7	7	7	7	7	7	7	7	7	7	7	8
8	8	8	8	8	8	8	8	8	8	8	8	8

Step 5

Color variations

For this variation I stuck to a more limited palette and worked with a range of oranges, purples and reds. The cool purples complement the warmth of the rich oranges.

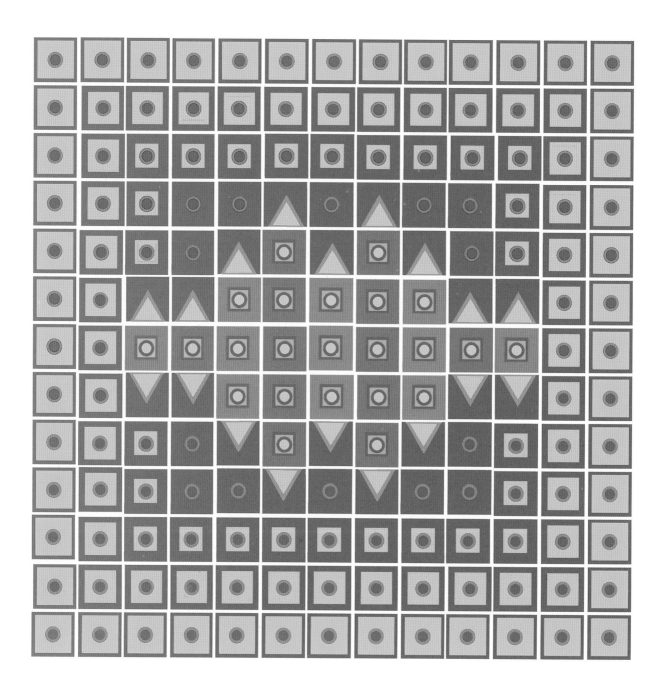

Color variations

Here is the ideal design for using up all those yarn odds and ends that you can't bear to part with. This psychedelic palette is a glorious riot of color, perfect for color-loving characters!

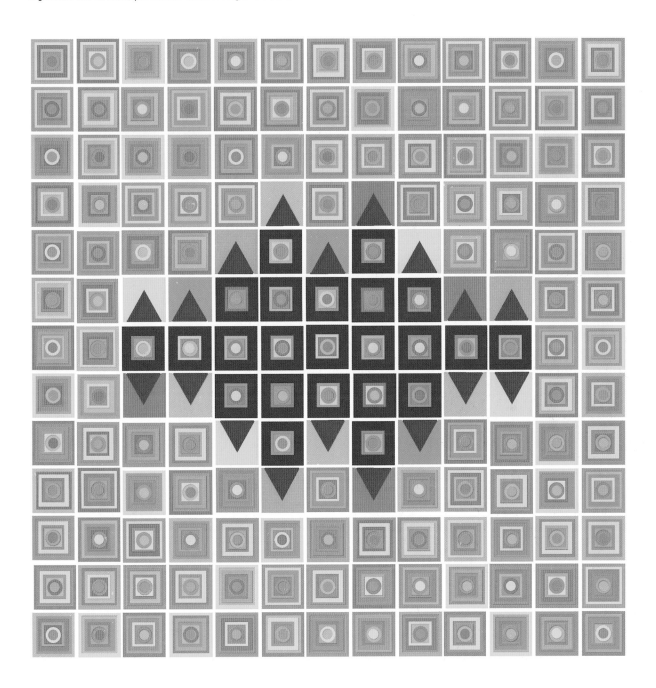

Flower Power

Flower Power, and its sister afghan Liberty on page 116, were originally inspired by an early morning summer walk along the West Lyn river in Exmoor, UK. I came across a small meadow on the bank of the river full of sparkling cobwebs and summer flowers. I took the two afghans in different directions: the colors here are taken from the bright and bold fabrics of the 1970s, hence the name 'flower power'.

Afghan size
50 x 58in (127 x 147.5cm)

Hook size
4mm (US G/6)

Yarn type
DK (8-ply) yarn: 263–273yd (240–250m) per 100g

Yarn notes
I made this afghan with oddments of yarn left over from other projects. If you prefer to buy new yarn, consider choosing the yarn brands below. You do not need to use the same dye lots.

Color palette

Use oddments and leftovers from other projects.

Gold: 150g   Orange: 150g   Soft red: 150g   Violet: 150g   Apple: 900g

Worldwide brands:
Cascade: 220 Sport
Knit Picks: Wool of the Andes Sport
Yarn Stories: Merino DK, Merino/Alpaca DK

UK independent dyers and spinners:
John Arbon Textiles: Knit by Numbers DK

Construction

Start at the center of the afghan and work outwards.

JOINING: The finished hexagons are slip stitched or crocheted together along each side. Crochet into the corresponding gaps between the stitches on each side of the motif.

FINISHING: To create a border, work two rows of single crochet.

Color chart

This chart is designed to give you an overall look at how this afghan is composed, and how the colors interact with each other; there is further detail on the afghan's motif arrangement in the step-by-step section (pages 112–113). The most prominent color here is green but you don't need to use the same colors as I have done. There are two other color variation charts for inspiration on pages 114 and 115.

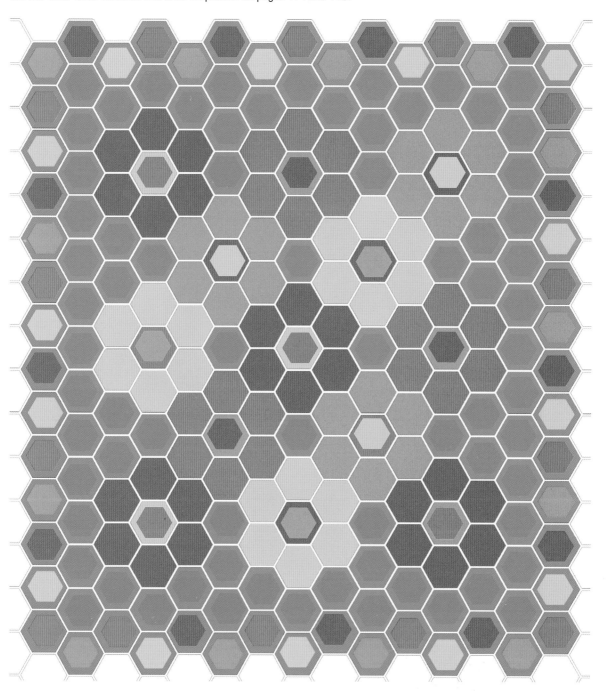

The motif arrangement

Hexagon motif

Each measures 2in (5cm) each side

Using color 1, make a 4-ch foundation chain and join in a ring with a sl st.

Round 1: 2 ch (counts as 1 hdc), 11 hdc in the foundation ring. Join to the 2nd st of original 2-ch with a sl st (12 hdc).

Round 2: in this and all following rounds work into the gaps between sts from the previous round, 2 ch (counts as 1 hdc), 1 hdc in same gap, *2 hdc in next gap*. Repeat from * to * 10 times. Join to the 2nd st of original 2-ch with a sl st (24 hdc).

Round 3: 2 ch (counts as 1 hdc), *1 hdc in next 3 gaps, (1 hdc, 2 ch**, 1 hdc) in next gap. Repeat from * to * 5 times ending last repeat at **. Join to the 2nd st of original 2-ch with a sl st. Fasten off.

Round 4: join color 2 in any 2-ch space, 2 ch (counts as 1 hdc), 1 hdc in same space, *2 ch, (2 hdc, 2 ch**, 2 hdc) in next 2-ch space*. Repeat from * to * 5 times ending last repeat at **. Join to the 2nd st of original 2-ch with a sl st.

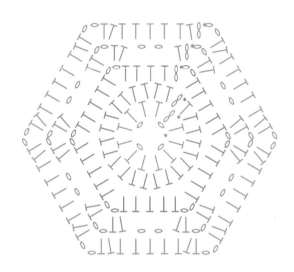

The motif stitch diagram

Round 5: 2 ch (counts as 1 hdc), 1 hdc in same space, *1 hdc in next gap, 3 hdc in the 2-ch space, 1 hdc in next gap, (2 hdc, 2 ch**, 2 hdc) in the 2-ch corner space*. Repeat from * to * 5 more times ending last repeat at **. Join to the 2nd st of original 2-ch with a sl st. Fasten off. Use the tail end to crochet or sew to the adjoining motif (9 hdc on each side of the hexagon).

The layout key

Motif	Rounds 1, 2 & 3	Rounds 4 & 5
Motif 1: make 2	Gold	Violet
Motif 2: make 2	Orange	Violet
Motif 3: make 3	Soft red	Gold
Motif 4: make 3	Violet	Orange
Motif 5: make 1	Orange	Soft red
Motif 6: make 1	Soft red	Orange
Motif 7: make 1	Gold	Soft red
Motif 8: make 24	Violet	Apple

Motif	Rounds 1, 2 & 3	Rounds 4 & 5
Motif 9: make 18	Orange	Apple
Motif 10: make 18	Gold	Apple
Motif 11: make 18	Soft red	Apple
Motif 12: make 72	Apple	Apple
Motif 13: make 14	Gold	Apple
Motif 14: make 13	Orange	Apple
Motif 15: make 14	Soft red	Apple
Motif 16: make 13	Violet	Apple

Making Flower Power

1 Start with the central flower. Take one Motif 3 hexagon and six Motif 8 hexagons, and slip stitch them together as shown.

2 Add another round of hexagons: slip stitch two Motif 10 hexagons, four Motif 9 hexagons, four Motif 12 hexagons and two Motif 11 hexagons in place as shown.

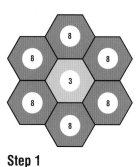

Step 1

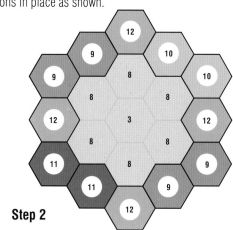

Step 2

3 Add another round of hexagons: take five Motif 11 hexagons, five Motif 10 hexagons, four Motif 9 hexagons, one Motif 1 hexagon, one Motif 2 hexagon, one Motif 4 hexagon, one Motif 7 hexagon and slip stitch them in place as shown.

4 Take two Motif 4 hexagons, six Motif 11 hexagons, six Motif 10 hexagons, four Motif 12 hexagons, four Motif 9 hexagons, one Motif 2 hexagon and one Motif 5 hexagon. Slip stitch them in place as shown to create the next round.

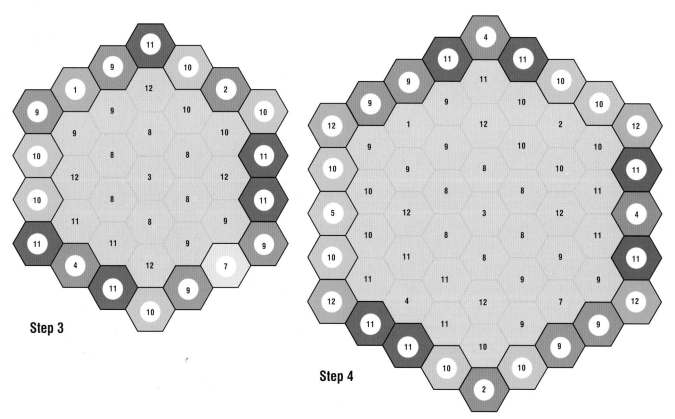

Step 3

Step 4

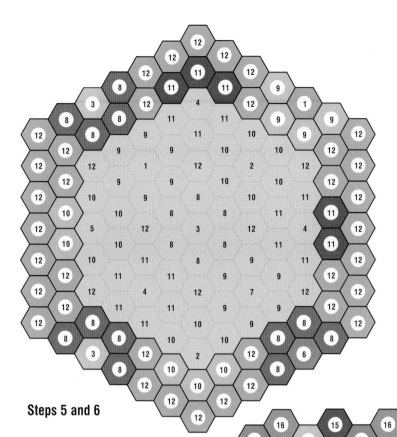

Steps 5 and 6

5 Continue to work a round at a time. Take five Motif 11 hexagons, twelve Motif 12 hexagons, two Motif 9 hexagons, six Motif 8 hexagons and five Motif 10 hexagons, and slip stitch in place as shown.

6 Slip stitch the next round of motifs in place as shown, using: twenty-four Motif 12 hexagons, two Motif 9 hexagons, one Motif 1 hexagon, six Motif 8 hexagons, one Motif 6 hexagon and two Motif 3 hexagons.

7 Complete the next round of hexagons, slip stitching them in place as shown: six Motif 15 hexagons, five Motif 14 hexagons, twelve Motif 12 hexagons, two Motif 9 hexagons, five Motif 16 hexagons, six Motif 13 hexagons, six Motif 8 hexagons.

8 To complete each corner of the rectangle, work one at a time, slip stitching the motifs in place in rows working outwards. In total you will need: sixteen Motif 12 hexagons, eight Motif 16 hexagons, eight Motif 14 hexagons, eight Motif 13 hexagons and eight Motif 15 hexagons.

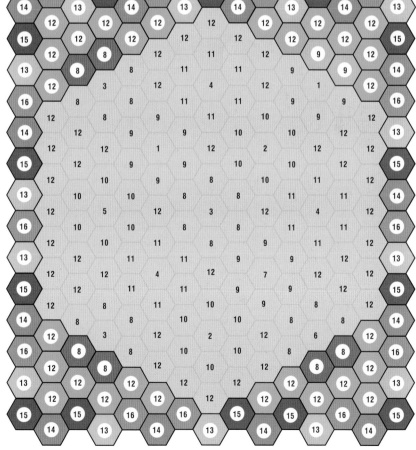

Steps 7 and 8

Color variations

Instead of using meadow greens as the main color of my afghan, here I used pinks and purples with a colorful arrangement of flowers in the center.

Color variations

Bright purples and calm yellows complement each other in this colorful, contemporary variation.

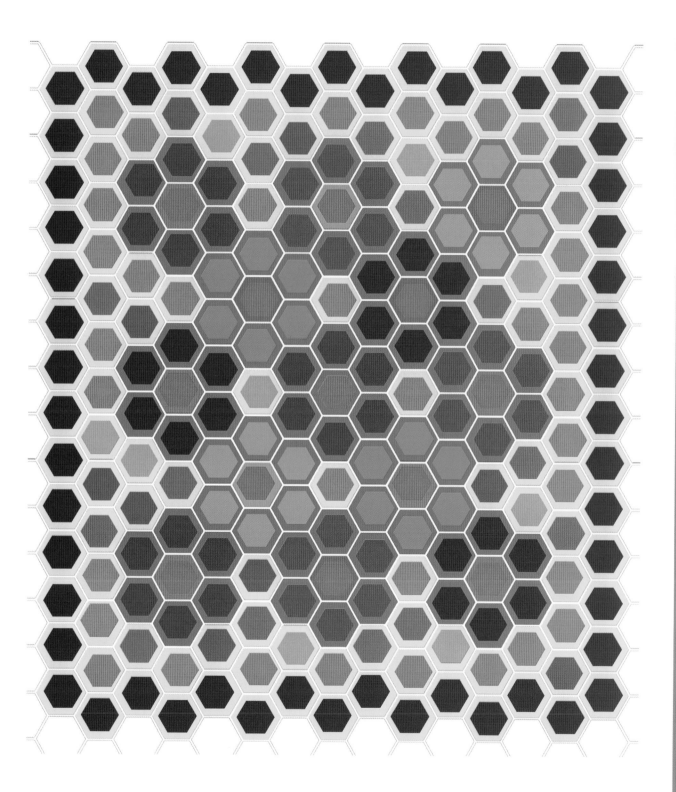

Liberty

On our riverside walk we passed through a meadow full of sparkling cobwebs, fairies – my children's name for dandelion and rose bay willow herb seeds – floating in the air, and summer flowers glistening in the morning sun. It was one of those magical moments in time. This is the second afghan of the pair, created as a direct contrast to Flower Power and inspired by subtle, elegant Liberty-print fabric.

Afghan size
50 x 60in (127 x 152.5cm)

Hook size
3 or 3.25mm (US C/2 or D/3)

Yarn type
Fingering (4-ply) yarn:
   390yd (360m) per 100g

Yarn notes
I made this afghan with oddments of yarn left over from other projects. If you prefer to buy new yarn, consider choosing the yarn brands below. You do not need to use the same dye lots.

Worldwide brands:
Drops: Alpaca, Alpaca/Silk
Fyberspates: Vivacious 4-ply
Cascade: 220 Fingering, Heritage Silk
Knit Picks: Palette yarn

UK independent dyers and spinners:
Skein Queen: Selkino, Lustrous
John Arbon Textiles: Exmoor Sock,
Knit by Numbers 4-ply
Easyknits: Splendour
The Little Grey Sheep: Stein 4-ply

Color palette

Use oddments and leftovers from other projects.

Orange: 100g   Soft red: 350g   Rose: 100g   Lilac: 200g   Azure: 100g

Green: 300g   Lime: 100g

Construction

Liberty is worked from side to side.

JOINING: The finished hexagons are slip stitched or crocheted together along each side. Crochet into the corresponding gaps between the stitches on each side of the motif.

FINISHING: Liberty doesn't have a border; if you choose to add one you might want to work two rows of half double crochet.

Color chart

This chart is designed to give you an overall look at how this afghan is composed, and how the colors interact with each other; there is further detail on the afghan's motif arrangement in the step-by-step section (pages 121–122). The most prominent color here is green but you don't need to use the same colors as I have done. There are two other color variation charts for inspiration on pages 124 and 125.

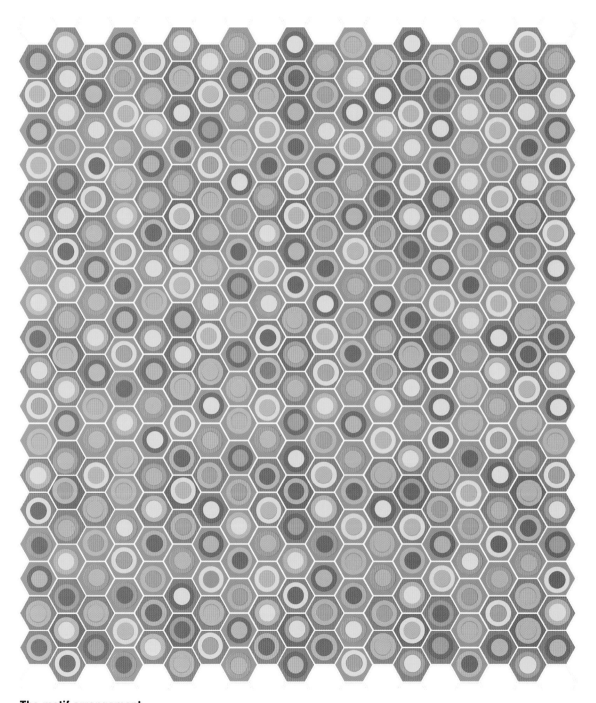

The motif arrangement

Hexagon motif

Measures 1½in (4cm) each side

Using color 1, make a 4-ch foundation chain and join in a ring with a sl st.

Round 1: 2 ch (counts as 1 hdc), 11 hdc in the foundation ring. Join to the 2nd st of original 2-ch with a sl st. Fasten off (12 hdc).

Round 2: in this and all following rounds work into the gaps between sts from the previous round. Join color 2 where round 1 completed, 2 ch (counts as 1 hdc), 1 hdc in same gap, *2 hdc in next gap*. Repeat from * to * 10 times. Join to the 2nd st of original 2-ch with a sl st (24 hdc). Fasten off.

Round 3: join color 3 where round 2 completed, 2 ch (counts as 1 hdc), *1 hdc in next 3 gaps, (1 hdc, 2 ch**, 1 hdc) in next gap. Repeat from * to * 5 times ending last repeat at **. Join to the 2nd st of original 2-ch with a sl st. Fasten off.

Round 4: join color 4 in any 2-ch space, 2 ch (counts as 1 hdc), 1 hdc in same space, *2 ch, (2 hdc, 2 ch**, 2 hdc) in next 2-ch space*. Repeat from * to * 5 times ending last repeat at **. Join to the 2nd st of original 2-ch with a sl st.

Round 5: 2 ch (counts as 1 hdc), 1 hdc in same space, *1 hdc in next gap, 3 hdc in the 2-ch space, 1 hdc in next gap, (2 hdc, 2 ch**, 2 hdc) in the 2-ch corner space*. Repeat from * to * 5 more times ending last repeat at **. Join to the 2nd st of original 2-ch with a sl st. Fasten off. Use the tail end to crochet or sew to the adjoining motif (9 hdc on each side of the hexagon).

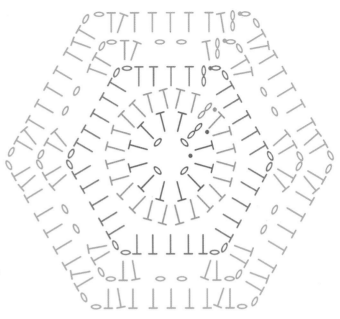

The motif stitch diagram

The layout key

Motif	Round 1	Round 2	Round 3	Round 4	Round 5
Motif 1: make 25	Orange, soft red, rose, lilac, azure, green or lime	Orange, soft red, rose, lilac, azure, green or lime	Orange, soft red, rose, lilac, azure, green or lime	Lilac	Lilac
Motif 2: make 150	Orange, soft red, rose, lilac, azure, green or lime	Orange, soft red, rose, lilac, azure, green or lime	Orange, soft red, rose, lilac, azure, green or lime	Soft red	Soft red
Motif 3: make 176	Orange, soft red, rose, lilac, azure, green or lime	Orange, soft red, rose, lilac, azure, green or lime	Orange, soft red, rose, lilac, azure, green or lime	Green	Green

Making Liberty

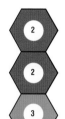

1 This afghan is constructed from side to side, working in columns. Start by slip stitching a column of motifs together, end to end. You will need: ten Motif 2 blocks and eight Motif 3 blocks.

Step 1

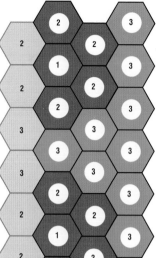

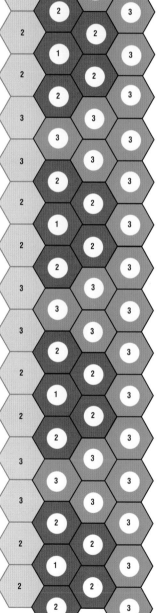

2 Continue to work across the afghan a column at a time. For the second column, take ten Motif 2 blocks, five Motif 1 blocks and four Motif 3 blocks. Slip stitch them in place as shown.

3 Column 3 is a repeat of column 1. Slip stitch ten Motif 2 blocks and eight Motif 3 blocks in place as shown.

4 Column 4 is composed entirely of nineteen Motif 3 blocks. Slip stitch them in place as shown.

Steps 2–4

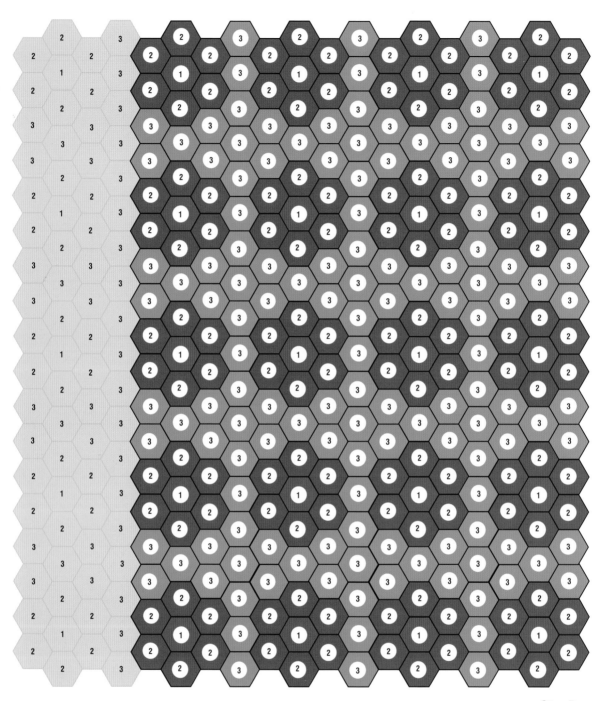

Step 5

5 The rest of the afghan repeats steps 1–4 but omits the final column of green. In total you will need twenty Motif 1 blocks, 120 Motif 2 blocks and 137 Motif 3 blocks. Slip stitch them in place a column at a time.

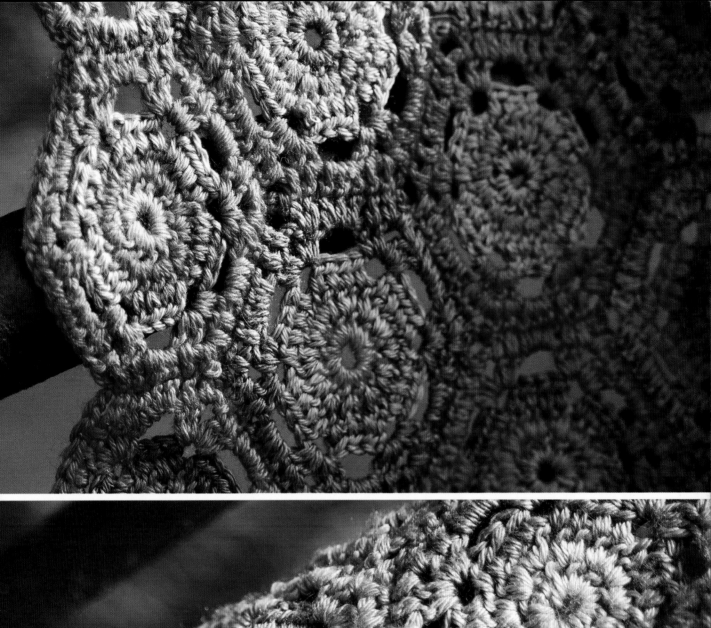

Color variations

For this variation I chose purple for my flowers, and soothing
blue and green tones for the surrounding background.

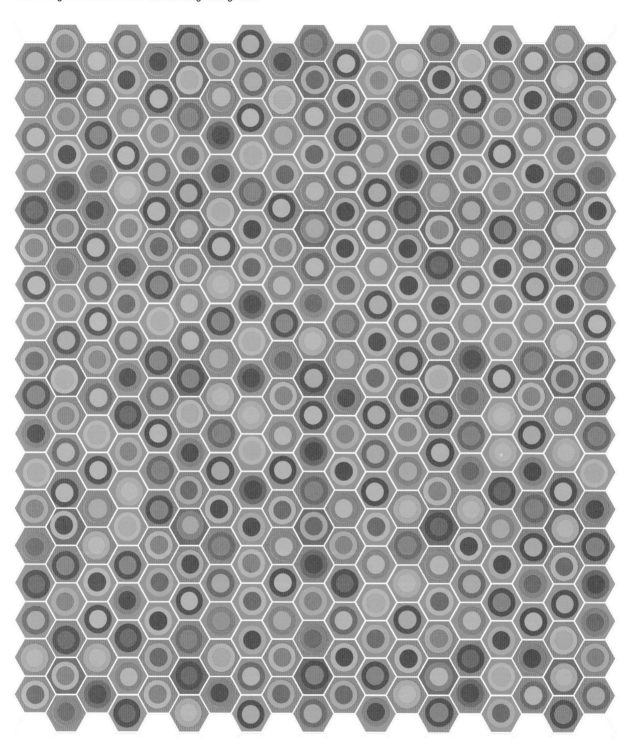

Color variations

For this variation, I imagined a summer garden in full, riotous color, and used a wide range of beautiful vibrant tones.